NATIVE AMERICAN HISTORY FOR KIDS

Explore Timeless Tales, Myths, Legends, Bedtime Stories & Much More from The Native Indigenous Americans

HISTORY BROUGHT ALIVE

© **Copyright 2023 - All rights reserved.**

The content contained within this book may not be reproduced, duplicated, or transmitted without direct written permission from the author or the publisher.

Under no circumstances will any blame or legal responsibility be held against the publisher, or author, for any damages, reparation, or monetary loss due to the information contained within this book, either directly or indirectly.

Legal Notice:

This book is copyright protected. It is only for personal use. You cannot amend, distribute, sell, use, quote, or paraphrase any part, or the content within this book, without the consent of the author or publisher.

Disclaimer Notice:

Please note the information contained within this document is for educational and entertainment purposes only. All effort has been executed to present accurate, up-to-date, reliable, complete information. No warranties of any kind are declared or implied. Readers acknowledge that the author is not engaged in the rendering of legal, financial, medical, or professional advice. The content within this book has been derived from various sources. Please consult a licensed professional before attempting any techniques outlined in this book.

By reading this document, the reader agrees that under no circumstances is the author responsible for any losses, direct or indirect, that are incurred as a result of the use of the information contained within this document, including, but not limited to, errors, omissions, or inaccuracies.

FREE BONUS FROM HBA: EBOOK BUNDLE

Greetings!

First of all, thank you for reading our books. As fellow passionate readers of History and Mythology, we aim to create the very best books for our readers.

Now, we invite you to join our VIP list. As a welcome gift, we offer the History & Mythology Ebook Bundle below for free. Plus you can be the first to receive new books and exclusives!
Remember it's 100% free to join.

Simply scan the QR code to join.

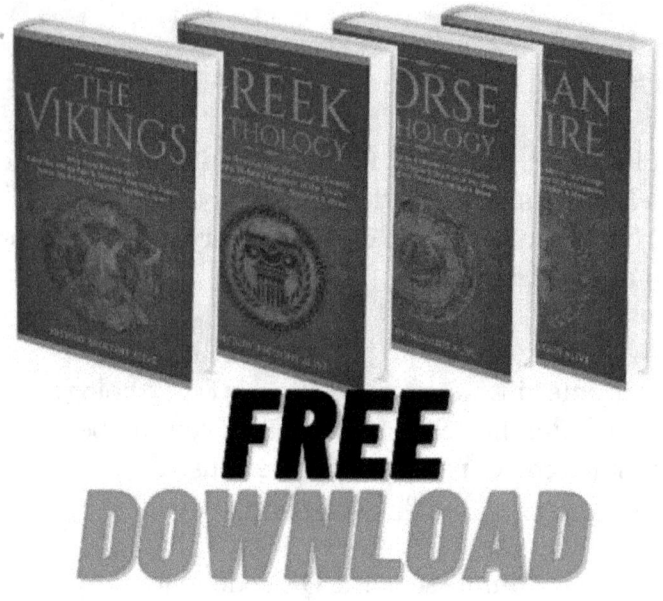

Keep up to date with us on:
YouTube: History Brought Alive
Facebook: History Brought Alive
www.historybroughtalive.com

CONTENTS

CHAPTER 1: INTRODUCTION TO NATIVE AMERICAN HISTORY 7

WHAT ARE NATIVE AMERICANS? 8
WHAT IS THE DIFFERENCE BETWEEN TRIBES AND CULTURES? 8
American Indian Communities......................*10*
HUNTING AS A LIFESTYLE 12
Conflict Occurred in Different Tribes 14
THE CONNECTIONS WITH THE PAST 15
Treaties Were No Substitute for Freedom......18
AMERICAN INDIAN CITIZENSHIP 25

CHAPTER 2: THE INUIT AND YUPIK GROUPS 27

BATHS AND HYGIENE 28
FAMILY AND MARRIAGE 34
When Your Dog Is the Only Transport...........37
Would Dogs Help in Times of Disaster?....... 39
THE CULTURAL AND BELIEFS OF AMERICAN INDIANS 41
Iglulik Religion 42
Netsilik Inuit 42
Angakkuq... 43
Moon Man.. 43
The Caribou Inuit 43
Spirits and Creatures 44
Tales the Communities Would Tell 45

CHAPTER 3: LIFE OF NATIVE AMERICANS 49

BATHS, KITCHENS, AND HYGIENE 53
   A Sweat Lodge *54*
   Ways of Cooking Different Dishes *57*
   Native American Dogs *60*
MARRIAGE AND FAMILY LIFE............................... 67
THE LANGUAGE THAT WAS SPOKEN 69
THE CULTURAL AND BELIEFS OF AMERICAN INDIANS.. 70
   Divine Help and Support in Everyday Matters *72*

CHAPTER 4: THREE FAMOUS NATIVE AMERICANS 77

POCAHONTAS.. 77
SACAGAWEA... 81
SITTING BULL 88

CHAPTER 5: NATIVE AMERICAN ARTS & CRAFTS 93

POTTERY... 93
   Mississippian Era *95*
   Cheyenne Earthenware *96*
   Pottery Shoshone *96*
   Cherokee Ceramic Work................................. *97*
   Ancient Pueblo Pottery *97*
   Navajo Indian Horsehair Ceramics *99*
   Iroquois Stoneware *99*
   Modern Native American Pottery *100*
BEADWORK...101
   Native American Culture..............................*101*
   Making Beads Out of Natural Materials *102*
   European Settlers Introduced a Style *103*

Weaving 107
   Finger Weaving *107*

CHAPTER 6: NATIVE AMERICAN GAMES AND SPORTS 113

Lacrosse.. 113
Shinny 116
Stickball... 119

CHAPTER 7: FAMOUS NATIVE AMERICAN LANDMARKS AND PLACES 123

Mesa Verde National Park 124
Chaco Canyon..128
Grand Canyon National Park...................... 135

CHAPTER 8: NATIVE AMERICAN TRIBES TODAY 141

Tribes That Still Exist Today 143
   The Cherokee Tribe...*144*
   The Navajo Tribe *147*
   The Latin American Indians *148*
   Choctaw Tribe *149*
Colonization Changed Eskimo Hunting 152
   Yupik Tribes..*155*
   How Can We Support Native American Communities..*160*

CONCLUSIONS 165

REFERENCES 171

INTRODUCTION

There is so much we are going to discover in this book about all the interesting American Native People that once stayed on this beautiful continent for all our recorded history.

In contrast to 'American Indian,' most people believe that 'Native American' is a favored term and it's polite, but this isn't actually the case. As a result, it is wrong to say anyone alive is a Native American.

The older, very rural, and far more reservation-based phrases are 'American Indian.' 'Indigenous,' has become a popular phrase during the past fifteen years. Sometimes the term 'Native' alone is used.

The Native tribes settled in North America, while the most radical hunter-gatherers in the world are populated in areas that we won't be able to stay in, such as the Inuit and Yupik tribes.

These remarkable and fascinating tribes still exist through the descendants that live on as the American Indian people in the United States today.

As I was saying, many tribes settled in the far North of Alaska. They covered a large span of countries all the way to the Gulf Coast in Florida, long before anyone else arrived in America. These Native tribes spread across hundreds of tribal nations and spoke hundreds of unique languages.

At one stage, there were over 300 written languages, and as many as 500 in total were spoken across the continent. The tribal people were fiercely loyal and active participants in their cultures and customs.

These people have a rich cultural religion that is filled with mythology, and they tell tales that have helped people live better lives. Some of these tales are quite amusing, and they help you consider situations and explain the best way forward. This book has some of those tales for you to read and enjoy!

Their religion, medicine, and way of life were one with nature. They created everything they needed, from what was available around them, by using their hands and minds. These tribes were and still are very talented people. They think differently from us and are very creative. This is seen in how they constructed large cities, created artwork, and lived healthy lifestyles.

They are true artists, and their talent is classified as the best in the world. We will have a look into their achievements with regard to pottery, beading, as well as weaving. These tribal people have also helped us develop the sports we play and watch today, and we will also read about these later.

The food they ate came from their kills by way of hunting and gathering berries, roots, and herbs, and eventually, they became farmers. In this book, we have the opportunity to discover these tribes and how they had to eat a varied diet in accordance with the climate. Tribal food choices and cooking style abilities are used as examples today. As the food they ate was a healthier approach to life. Several Native American tribes carried out farming activities and produced the crops we often eat today. Their culture has never hindered their progress, and now there are American Indians that are participating in every walk of life.

Some have followed a Western path and become doctors, lawyers, chartered accountants, and wealthy businesspeople. Yet many have stayed true to their customs and traditions and have chosen to uphold the legacy of thousands of generations.

We will read that in one moment, everything changed for the Native Americans, and their foundation started to crack as the European settlers arrived. At first, promises were made, but none were upheld.

Both sides fought viciously for what they held dear or precious, and many lives were lost and destroyed. Terrible systems were put in place that threatened everything the Native American tribes stood for and believed in.

Youngsters were all sent to Indian boarding schools, where they were taught an English culture and given a European education. The government integration program got rid of most of the languages, and today they no longer exist.

Nowadays, tribal members number over twelve million people, and they live in the present-day United States. Don't you think it's important to understand the history of America and those who live on the continent?

In winter, tribes had dwellings that kept the cold out, and they made provisions to store food or hunt certain animals in the season. Where do your ancestors come from? Are you an

American Indian, or does your family originate from Europe, or did you recently arrive from the East?

We will walk through the decades together, from when everyone first arrived in the United States. Following that, we will find out how the tribal people built their houses and hunted. We will also read many stories about creation and the Native Americans' way of life before and after the arrival of the Europeans.

For instance, we will find out what Andrew Jackson agreed to as he signed the Indian Removal Act in 1830. Do you know that Native People were forcibly removed from their homes and relocated to reservations in the 1800s?

This act came about from the Europeans wanting to cultivate cotton in the South and dig out gold in the North. These were the main driving forces for this disgraceful behavior when moving these original land dwellers off their lands. Tribes such as Choctaw, Creek, Cherokee, and others really suffered in this move (Cyca, 2022).

Native People were forcibly removed from Alabama, Florida, Georgia, North Carolina, and Tennessee and sent to 'Indian territory' in what is now known as Oklahoma. Thousands died on these marches, and many more tribes were forcibly moved by the U.S. government. They were left without anywhere to go and no territory of their own.

Only 22% of Native Americans are living on tribal territory today, according to statistics taken in 2010. The U.S. Department of Housing and Urban Development found in a 2014 research that 68% of American Indians and Alaskan Natives stay on or close to their ancestral grounds (Cyca, 2022).

We are also going to look at areas or places that the Native Americans kept as sacred ground. We are also going to look into ways of helping the present-day American Indian to acquire a better way of life. Let's not wait; come on, read with me!

CHAPTER 1
INTRODUCTION TO NATIVE AMERICAN HISTORY

What do you think when you hear the word Eskimo? Maybe you imagined people wearing thick furry clothes surrounded by snow. Most of the areas the Eskimos live in have snow for eight months of the year. Playing in the snow is fun, but can you imagine living in those conditions?

In this chapter, we will learn about the fascinating beginnings of the Native tribes that settled in America many years ago—one being the Inuit hunter-gatherer. The word 'Inuit' means the indigenous 'Eskimo.' These were populations that settled in Northern Alaska, Chukotka, Canada, and Greenland.

The other main group of Eskimos is mainly towards the West, and they are known as the Yupik group. Today some of the Yupik tribe also live in Alaska, while others stay on St. Lawrence Island, the Diomede Islands, and in Russia. They share cultural ties with the Canadian Chukchi and Inuit, as well as the Kalaallit Nunaat from Greenland.

What Are Native Americans?

Native Americans are recognized as the Indigenous or the first peoples of the U.S. mainland. They are also called American Indians, Indigenous Americans, Cree, and many other titles.

We also need to understand that these tribes are rooted in their culture and their love for nature. It has been well documented throughout history and is still true now how important the environment is to Indian American culture.

The natural world touches every part of their culture--religion, customs, mythology, literature, food, art, medicine, and much more.

When you understand the importance of nature in Native American culture, you will notice that every idea they have had previously, and still have today, has taken over every kind of artwork they have produced.

What is the Difference Between Tribes and Cultures?

Clan or close-knit members often take on a

particular collective culture they agree with. 'Culture' is a general term used to explain group interaction (working together), traditions, and values in human societies or tribes.

It also explains the people that make up these communities as well as their knowledge, abilities, and beliefs. Culture is frequently said to have started in a certain area or has been influenced by a particular area or place.

The tribes, on the other hand, are a wider social group to which the clan members belong. A tribe often stands out as a distinct group that belongs to one culture but doesn't always follow one culture completely. A tribe often has a few distinctive qualities that stand out and ties them together.

Our American history is significantly affected by the indigenous people that have settled in the states. It also helps us to understand how we arrived and where we are today. It can also foster friendly neighbors as it instills respect for differences or diversity in people. Additionally, it creates an understanding of the wide range of skills and interests that exist. Providing a head start to respect and value intellectual outputs as we understand past cultures and tribes. Further, it leads to an understanding of different people, creating a stable, well-rounded nation. Which provides comprehensive perspectives and a gauge of what is lasting in the life of a country.

In fact, understanding our past from a historical viewpoint act as a compass, and it often shows us what can be expected or what is to come in the future. We can learn from the past, and we can decide what will be the best path to follow. It helps us see what we should take with us into the future or what needs to be dumped.

It's similar to when you learned the stove was hot as a child, history tells you what happens when you do, and you won't easily touch it again. This in no way suggests that individuals have no free will.

American Indian Communities

The next group we need to investigate is the American Indian communities in North America. Have you ever played 'Cowboys and Indians' with your friends? I can remember those game sets that we used to buy, with headpieces and bows and soft nose arrows and plastic guns and a cowboy hat. If you answered yes to the question, the Cowboys and Indians you used to act out when playing your games were this next group.

These nomadic hunters came from Northeast Asia, and they are thought to give rise to the American Indians, who seemed to have crossed the Bering Straits, a land bridge, entering North America from the northern parts of Alaska.

This happened at some point during the last glacial period (11,500 to 30,000 years ago). These tribes took over a large portion of North and South America and the central parts by 10,000 BC. The members of the indigenous tribes that stayed in the region were generally bordered on the North side.

This was because of the largely changeable landscape that was primarily deciduous woodland, which moved into taiga (high Northern areas with marshy evergreen) woodland, in the East by the Atlantic Ocean; in the West by the Mississippi River valley; and in the South to an extent, that was the area that extended from the coast of modern-day Carolina to the North West on the Ohio River; and from there Southwest to its meeting up with the Mississippi River, at the time of European arrival.

The cultural region of the Northeast is made up of a variety of temperate wetlands, woods, meadows, waterways, as well as coastal regions.

This area was inhabited by many different groups, each belonging to the Algonquian, Iroquoian, or Siouan tribes, as reported by European explorers and colonists in the 16th century.

We know what land was used by the Indians because there is a lot of proof that has been written down, which has supported their lifestyle. There has also been proof of the terrible hardships or suffering that these tribes had gone through and have been forced to live under. I will explain further as I zone in on the encounters of the Native Americans and the Europeans (Westerners etc.) or the Anglo-American settlers that came to North America.

Hunting as a Lifestyle

When hunting is your life, killing is necessary. Yet to these tribes, non-violence is a precious virtue when preserving civilization. The men in the Eskimo tribes need to be self-sufficient and good hunters in order to be effective or good providers. Yet, they also need to be nurturing to fit in with the group.

The Inuit adore hunting—their eyes light up with delight when they share hunting tales. Hunting has always been a way of life, and it means success, yet these tribes associate aggression with danger, and they will try on all accounts to avoid it.

Conflict or unrest within the community was seldom heard of, and opposing ideas were unusual in the Eskimo groups. In fact, the tribes respond with shock to any form of shouting or aggressiveness when it's aimed at another person.

They viewed aggression so seriously that they adopted a system to prevent conflict. For instance, they never showed pride or bragged about themselves but acted humbly, and they treated everyone equally within the community.

They never ask direct questions but hint at suggestions or joke about atopic. They don't promise anything, and they don't invite people to any future events or outings. They will never force anyone into a situation but act peacefully, and they allow one another enough space. If anyone gets angry, they will simply walk away from the situation.

If a community member battles with anger and fails to control themselves, the community will ostracize or avoid that person. The person will not be included in any activities until they gain control of their anger.

The community will continually show warmth and love, and kindness towards community members. They will always help those that need it, but aggression and anger have never been tolerated. Wouldn't it be a wonderful world if we all tried not to argue and fight?

Conflict Occurred in Different Tribes

There have always been conflicts, as tribes have worked to resolve situations. However, the Inuit, Yupik, and the smaller groups of the Central and Eastern Canadian Arctic, such as the Utku and Qipisa groups, have historically worked hard to control their anger.

They don't show much gender (male and female) related stress or conflict either. Families don't seem to fight at all; in fact, they nurture and watch over one another. There is a sense of tranquility and warmth within an Eskimo's home and a sensitivity to the hidden needs of family members.

Yet, the Eskimos have gone to war, both in prehistoric times and well into the era following the European settlement. This is especially true with the Indians living in the Southern regions.

Throughout the 17th and 18th centuries, Europeans were busy with the fur trade forts on each side of the Hudson Bay and James Bay area. In those areas, battles were documented, or described in writing, between the local Cree Indians from the South and the Inuit tribes from the North.

The Connections With the Past

All American Natives, or indigenous tribes, are descended from people that used to be simple hunters and gatherers, just like everyone else in the world. Tribal people would often keep up their hunting and gathering ways as a regular backup plan for times of shortages. In other words, hunting would extend as a supplement to those who worked other types of jobs.

According to the American Indians, the term 'family' includes the extended family, tribal community, and the current American Indian population as a whole. It also includes members of blood-related and unrelated groups.

As the American Indians believe, they come from one original group of ancestors. In this sense, living as an American Indian means—a person is never actually alone or without family or blood relatives.

All that an American Indian stood for—and many still stand for—had been affected by the Europeans' arrival that came from the North. The American Indians fought viciously to keep what they had and tried to push the Europeans out of the land. The relationship structure between European settlers and the Indigenous populations that came across from North America was always tense, to say the least, as relations were not good.

The Europeans and Native Americans all started off by trying to work together; then it moved to fighting; whether they were the English, French, or Vikings, their actions all followed the same pattern. Yet the Pueblos of New Mexico became the exception! Although they were recorded as acting in a violent manner, in other similar situations before. The Pueblos showed hospitality and kindness to the Spanish people, who didn't show the same kindness in return.

Today, we can honestly state that Native ideas have enriched and added to conversations on social, economic, as well as political issues.

What Is a Promise Without Following Through?

The budding American Republic swore to treat the original rulers of the territory or those that occupied the land, such as the American Indian land-dwellers, with kindness and fairness. Many statements were made, saying that the Europeans would be fair to the tribes. They also claimed peace and that they owed the American Indian a duty of confidence or relaxation in this regard.

The Europeans made a few tries to keep their promises, but these 'good intentions' were undermined or worn away by their basic misunderstanding of Native traditions. The Europeans looked down on the American Indians' beliefs when they took over, claiming "what was best for the Native People." These actions triggered unrest and brought on the repeat of wars.

Native Indians once lived in a large area of America long before the arrival of Christopher Columbus. These so-called Native people are now called the Americas.

As more explorers attempted to occupy the territory in the 16th and 17th centuries, the Native Americans reacted in a variety of different ways. These ranged from goodwill–to outrage or great anger–to revolution–which was a violent way to end a way of life or rule.

The American Indians are currently estimated to be between twelve and fifteen million people that are living in the United States (Wikipedia Contributors, 2019a).

Treaties Were No Substitute for Freedom

In the 1600s, treaties were written stating that large areas of land were given to the American Indians. Yet these treaties were never taken seriously. The lives and existence of the Native people have been held back by government policy since the Royal Proclamation of 1763.

To protect their culture and fight the invasion of their territory during the American Revolution, most American Indigenous Peoples joined forces with the British. Even so, some tribal people backed the Patriots to protect their cause due to interpersonal relationships, religious ties, or perhaps past British injustice. Many members of the Oneidas, Mohicans, Tuscaroras, and Stockbridge-Munsee Nations were among these allies (Wikipedia Contributors, 2019a).

Nonetheless, despite these acts, Native Americans have always fought to live their lives on their own terms and to uphold the freedom of their tribes as distinct rulers under the U.S. federal government and countries within a nation.

The days of the law have consistently changed between trying to "civilize" or change the Indian nation. The U.S. has promoted self-government and self-rule. Yet, in the past, conflict and wars carried on, and these brought a lot of violence and death to everyone.

Wars Between the American Indians and the Europeans

The main wars started in 1675, with King Philip's War, through to the final massacre or slaughter of the Indians in 1911. Early colonization through boarding schools took place. This boarding school policy was based on Richard Henry Pratt's Carlisle's 'Indian Industrial School' (Wikipedia Contributors, 2019a).

With this idea, Pratt thought that boarding schools would improve situations. Indian children were taken and raised in the "American way." These poor children were separated from their community and families and changed, so they became more like the Europeans, and they no longer had any Indian Native traces in them.

This made the American Indians upset and aggressive, as their families were being pulled apart, and their cultures and religions were being destroyed. This system the Europeans used was known as 'education for extinction.'

The takeover of Alcatraz Island (off the coast of San Francisco and California) in 1969. American Indian cultures felt strongly about their religion—which was a key part of their fighting. Two main examples of these battles were the Ghost Dance that occurred from 1889 to 1890 and the Pontiac's Rebellion (Wikipedia Contributors, 2019a).

The American Indians' heritage and their own forefathers date back thousands of years. Their culture had been established well before the arrival of Europeans. The Indian American's way of life has been a great part of the American tale right from the beginning.

Many Indians would also attack the Europeans when their families got sick, as they believed that the Europeans brought all these illnesses with them. The other reason why the American Indians launched raids toward the North was that warriors received fame when they fought the Europeans.

Even though these weren't the main reasons for the raids, the warriors' reputations grew to be a key secondary reason for their attacks. Also, the raids resulted in captured people, often women and children, and this provided a financial incentive (money gain) when the people were sold as slaves.

However, the Cree raids carried on despite the American Indians having no intention of taking over more territory. The Comanche tribe, among other American tribes, had a long history of abducting or kidnapping women and children from their enemies, such as the Europeans.

The tribal Indians sold the hostages they kidnapped in raids as slaves by taking them South to their settlements. Occasionally, the HBC would pay for the prisoners and release them to ensure that they wouldn't be killed.

This was definitely not a one-sided situation! The days of European history concerning Native American slavery have been swept under the carpet. Approximately 12.5 million enslaved Africans were held in American prisons from 1492 to 1880, and a further 2 million to 5.5 million Native American Indians were captured and held as slaves (Wikipedia Contributors,

2019b). After King Philip's era, massive amounts of tribal Americans were enslaved. Yet, Native Indians were forced into slavery as early as 1636 (Wikipedia Contributors, 2019b).

In those uncertain times, European prisoners were also seen as useful laborers who would be exchanged for valuable items. Captives often ended up becoming full-fledged tribal members, especially if they were stolen as young toddlers or children.

I am glad we don't live in those times anymore. It must have been terrible for those people to be separated from family and have so many die. Below let's look at the sad story of Cynthia Ann Parker's life as she landed in one of these situations.

Cynthia Ann Parker

Cynthia Ann Parker, also known as Naduah (the Comanche name), was a white lady who is known to have been kidnapped by a Comanche war party at around the age of nine during the Fort Parker massacre when she was adopted into the American Indian tribe. Cynthia lived from October 28, 1827, to March 1871. She had been abducted after a raid on her family ranch, and she was the only survivor after her family was brutally murdered.

After four years, at the Canadian River in Northern Texas, a merchant by the name of Williams claimed to have seen a white girl with a group of Comanche. He made an unsuccessful attempt to buy her release. Williams was given permission by Comanche Chief Pahauka to speak to Cynthia, but she only stared at the ground and refused to speak back. Cynthia didn't seem to want Willian, or any other person sent to rescue her. She had clearly grown up in the Comanche culture, and she loved it there.

On another occasion, when white men saw Cynthia in 1845, she was about 17 years old at the time. The men both said, "she is unwilling to leave," and that she would run off and hide to avoid being taken when they tried to ransom her (History, 2023). Afterward, a Comanche warrior informed them they must leave, as she was his wife.

Peta Nocona, Cynthia's husband, treated her well, and the couple was very happy together. Nocona was apparently so happy with her that he refused the custom of taking many wives and having multiple children. It was obvious that Cynthia had decided that she was a Comanche. Cynthia's Parker gave birth to three children, two boys, and a girl.

Nocona and the rest of his tribe carried on

organizing several successful raids against the Europeans. In his own way, he kept up his bloody battle against the Anglo-American invaders. Peta Nocona was eventually murdered after Texas Rangers had enough of being attacked. Ranger troops invaded Nocona's settlement in December 1860. Nocona was fatally wounded, and the invading troops took Cynthia and her daughter Prairie Flower, into custody (Grimm, 2018).

After being forcibly returned to Anglo society, Cynthia was sent to her uncle's farm in Birdville, Texas. There, she repeatedly tried to run away, but she was always unsuccessful.

Cynthia experienced a great deal of heartbreak while living at her uncle's farm. First, she heard her husband died, and shortly after that, her daughter, Prairie Flower passed away from pneumonia and influenza. Cynthia's spirit seemed to be broken.

She no longer understood the people she stayed with, and she had no purpose and felt tired of life. Cynthia lived for another seven years while feeling depressed and alone. Sadly, she was weak due to malnutrition as she often stopped eating, and in 1870 she also passed away from influenza (History, 2023).

American Indian Citizenship

These first Americans were not made U.S. citizens until 1924, and shockingly this fact was frequently shared as a joke. Yet, the Indian Citizenship acted as a mere "clean-up stage," that applied to only a third of Native American people who hadn't become citizens yet. American Indians have always been and will always be a key part of American history.

The Supreme Court's 2020 judgment in McGirt v. Oklahoma made sure that a large portion of the nation would stay as Indian land or reservations due to various treaties that were originally negotiated between Native tribes at the time. The U.S. government tied the treaty to Jonas Michalius' letter, which was written in 1628, as proof (Acemoglu et al., 2001).

In 1793, the ethnic conflict and fighting suddenly stopped due to a shifting (moving) economy. The HBC posts were being filled with paid Cree tribes that helped with loading and transporting supplies as the companies grew to compete with rival merchants from the Northwestern Company.

The Cree or American Indians discovered that their occupations took up the majority of their summers, as the corporation needed a growing number of workers. The lives of the

American Indians changed, and they became financially secure as a result of the growing workload and income as the customer's needs increased. In other words, any extra financial needs incurred by the American Indians were supplemented with their traps and goose-shooting (Acemoglu et al., 2001).

In the next chapter, we are going to open up the climatic habitat of ancient cultures and how the American Indians lived or established themselves.

CHAPTER 2
THE INUIT AND YUPIK GROUPS

The Inuit and Yupik groups are known to be the most extreme examples of hunter-gatherers in the world. These robust groups of people relied mostly on hunting to survive in the world's toughest regions, and they targeted mainly marine creatures for their survival.

These amazing tribes are semi-nomadic groups of people who establish seasonal camps. This means that throughout the summer, the Eskimos live in tents that are made out of bone, animal hides, and driftwood.

In the winter months, they build igloos, or ice dwellings, which need a great deal of skill to make. These ice homes actually shelter the tribes from the cruel sub-degree arctic winds during the winter months.

Sadly these ice dwellings only last a short

period of the year because they melt in the warmer months. Can you imagine your family building a house every winter? Well, some tribes have become so good at building ice igloos that they can build one the size of a small house within an hour or two (Encyclopædia Britannica, 2019).

An Igloo Dwelling

Baths and Hygiene

Mukee is an ancient bathing process within Eskimo tribes. Tribe created a system to bathe that would use as little water as possible in an area where water is frozen for most of the year.

These tribes created an ingenious steam room. In addition to getting cleaner than what a shower can achieve, a steam bath also gives you a chance to interact with friends and family.

The steam room they created was compact. It was a two-room structure made of wood or logs and had 6-foot-high ceilings. A wood stove was positioned in a hollowed-out area on the floor. The smaller room is used to change out of or into clothes, and it can also be used to cool down once leaving the steam room. You can only sit or lie down in the steam room because of the low ceilings.

I wonder if you would like to experience a muk'ee steam bath? I think it could be rather fun, though I'm not sure if I could cope with all that heat, could you? Usually, in a traditional muk'ee, the men first steam together and turn the woodstove as hot as it will go. The room's temperature could reach 150°F or more! The Inuit tribes have a challenge, "how hot can you steam," which tests the Eskimo's 'machismo side.'

The muk'ee is a social experience where people connect and have a lot of fun. When the steam bath becomes unbelievably hot, the woodstove literally rocks. This happens as the ferocious combustion, or burning, forces build up inside the stove. The stove pipes glow red hot, and the red-hot heat color goes almost all the way to the ceiling.

Once the heat reaches that boiling point, all

the laughing and conversation stops. There is an eerie silence as each person focuses on getting through the furnace stage. As the person organizing the steam room begins to pour ladles of liquid over the woodstove, everyone lies flat on the floor to allow the steam to billow overhead. This steam adds to the heat, but it also makes it easier to breathe.

Your skin begins tingling everywhere; this is especially so with the part of your body that faces the woodstove. Sweat begins to pour from every cell in your body. Your face is usually against the wall at this stage, and you try not to breathe on any part of your skin because your breath burns.

When it gets too hot, you can ask to leave the room; the door is opened quickly, and you swiftly exit; then the door is shut again before too much heat is lost. You can recover and take a seat in the changing area when the heat gets too much for you.

It is important to know when to leave the room and to make sure you drink enough water in the course of the day, as the steam room causes a large loss of body fluid. If the individual doesn't drink enough water, dehydration takes place; this can lead to headaches for several hours after having a steam bath. The terrible headaches are not unusual, especially for the men in the tribe.

This steam room cleans from the inside out. The last stage is to clean up with soap and shampoo and a gallon of water. Wow! You are left with muk'ee fresh, clean skin. You also have a lacy design of redness all over your body to go along with it. This lacy pattern is known as reticularis livedo (Medlineplus, n.d.), and it's temporary marking; however, over time, a permanent pigment loss often takes place.

Making Tools and Hunting and Gathering

Traditional Inuit cuisine is described as being suitable for dignified people. It also contained plant life, such as roots and berries. Some of the traditional Inuit meats were Arctic char, polar bear, shellfish, seal, and caribou, which are often eaten raw, frozen, or dried.

The regional cuisine or food is rich in minerals and nutrients that people require to stay nourished during the difficult winter months. They also ate birds, eggs, and land animals, such as ducks, bears, ptarmigans, muskox, and caribou. The word 'country food' is broadly used; however, Inuit prefer to describe their Native cuisine as 'Tapiriit Kanatami.'

When looking for food, the Inuit gather or forage, trap, fish, and hunt. When the food was prepared, the tribes used tools such as the ulu, which is a type of knife. When available, the tribal people used stone and driftwood to make tools, along with bone or walrus ivory. These tribal people created harpoons and spears to hunt marine creatures such as seals and whales. Would you like to eat with the Eskimos?

Ptarmigans Hen

Amazing Finds

Amazingly, every part of what the tribes hunted is used by the Inuit, if not for food, then for other needs; animal hides and furs are used in clothing; fuel or seal oil is used for warmth; and bones and sinew are used in the building of many traditional tools. Even the partially digested plant meals found in a caribou stomach are eaten by some of these communities.

Archaeologists, people who study human history, discovered evidence of a 'Meteorite Era,' when prehistoric hunters in Greenland gathered metal debris that had fallen from the sky. The tribal people used these found materials to create weapons. A meteorite is a very hard material and makes ideal tools, according to evidence discovered by Danish researchers (Chahira, 2008).

Preparing Meals

Depending on cultural traditions and individual preferences, the tribes prepare a meal in many different ways. It might be eaten fresh, fried, salted, dried, fermented, or frozen.

Muktuk (or maktaaq) is the national dish eaten and is made up of strips of whale skin with fat. This meat would frequently come from a beluga, narwhal, or bowhead whale. Muktuk is often served uncooked and is a fantastic source of vitamin C.

Natural food creates a special connection between the Inuit and nature in a spiritual sense. It ties people to the planet, the creatures that live on it, the seas, and one another. Living off the land is another way to show gratitude to the animal who was hunted, as it gave its life so many could live.

Family and Marriage

There was a strong feeling of peace, warmth, and comfort in an Inuit home, as well as a sensitivity or a deep feeling within the family. There are certain duties given to men and women. The men did the dangerous and challenging hunting, and the women took care of the lighter physical chores, which included gathering food, cooking, watching the kids, and sewing.

Both partners would acknowledge the importance of each other's efforts; neither could survive without the other's provision. Each member was treated with respect and honored for what they did.

Infants are always cuddled and cherished, and children are never punished. The next child usually arrives when the youngster is three years old. This timing between having children was used as an emotional fitting-in in hopes that a child finds their position in the family.

The Inuit practice a type of 'benevolent aggression.' For instance, they explain to the child or person committing the 'crime'; that they are actually hurting themselves rather than inflicting pain on others, and they call it self-endangering.

In this way, they try to promote healthy social bonds. In a strange "act of violence," they show their children affection—by overfeeding them, roughhousing them as they nurse, and so forth—they cause ambivalence, meaning neither right nor wrong in their offspring toward both love and fear. They believe that these methods support a child's development, encourage independence, and instill apprehension and caution in the way their offspring see interpersonal relationships.

This behavior can occur when relationships between two or more individuals are mutual. This is a general term describing how people live in close quarters throughout the world. It relates to the different ways that individuals interact and communicate with one another directly.

A men's common house, or qasgiq, is where the males or fathers teach their sons life lessons. This includes survival and hunting techniques, in addition to rites and festivals. Religious shamans often participate, and rituals are held during the cold qasgiq trips.

Normally, the ena, or women's common house, was just next door. Sometimes the two groups shared houses that were linked by a tunnel. Little girls were taught by women or their mothers how to loom or weave, cook and prepare game and fish, and tan skins. Young boys would stay with their mothers up to the age of five; after that, they would join the men in the qasgiq.

The girls and the boys would then trade cultural teaching methods for a period of three to six weeks. For instance, the men would teach the girls survival and hunting methods as well as toolmaking. The women would also teach the boys what they were skilled in, so both genders (men and women) became completely independent.

There are stories that have surfaced from the past of elderly people being put outside in the cold of winter to die. The practice was finally put to an end, as pressure was applied from missionaries as well as national authorities to improve economic situations. A change happened in their thoughts of what was good behavior among Native peoples.

The terrible practice was, however, extremely uncommon and happened before 1939, when the final occurrence was reported. Whatever the situation, it is wrong to take anyone's life away from them.

The killing of elderly individuals, known as senicide, was never common among Eskimos. In the American Natives, it was widespread, but it was mostly among Inuit tribes rather than the Yuit tribes that were situated in Greenland.

An Inuit Figurine

When Your Dog Is the Only Transport

The tribes initially struggled because they needed to move around a lot to hunt and collect new supplies. Since they lacked transportation—no transport at all, not even bikes or motorcycles.

They got the idea to build sleds and use arctic, or polar, dogs to solve that problem. The end game is the tribes have trained dogs to drag or pull a sled that is laden with stuff they need to hunt or build with. Have you had fun on a sled in the snow? Let's have a look at how these sled dogs work in a team.

Every sled has a team of dogs, and they have a lead dog, or occasionally two. This dog leads the team fearlessly. Lead dogs, like the well-known Balto we are going to read about, must be quick and intelligent in order to properly pace and lead the team to victory. Swing dogs follow closely behind the lead dogs and help the team in 'swinging,' which means turning the corners and curves. The wheel dogs make up the largest and most powerful of the dogs as they pull the sled from the very back. Their responsibility is to pull the sled out of tricky areas where there are trees and problems, and this is where strength is needed. The final group of dogs is stationed in the middle, and they are referred to as team dogs. These dogs run where they are directed and pull the load together. The amount of sled dogs used will determine the dogs' power in a team when pulling a sled.

I would like to ride on a sled pulled by a team of dogs. I am sure it would be a lot of fun if you knew how!

Sled Dogs

Would Dogs Help in Times of Disaster?

All animals are a gift, and it's precious to own one. The people in the Inuit tribes depend on their dogs for basically everything. The dogs are just as tough as the climate and the Eskimos themselves. Why don't we read an extraordinary story from the past about these amazing animals?

There were a lot of outbreaks of terrible diseases in the early days, and diphtheria was one of them. This disease is highly contagious—this means anyone can catch it, and it spreads easily as COVID-19 did.

Diphtheria is a fatal illness if not treated quickly, and many people die from it. It starts off by affecting the throat and lungs, and you can't eat, and eventually, you can't breathe.

On January 20, 1925, doctors in the outlying Alaskan settlement of Nome found many cases of this illness in the Inuit tribe. The only way to save the village was to get a batch of serum in Alaska, as the weather was at its worst. Not to mention it was also 700 miles away from Anchorage. There was a pilot that helped fly in cases like this, but he was far away on another serious mission to the South, and he couldn't be back in time. This seemed like an impossible task as their only choice of transport was their dogs, but they had to try; getting the medication was the only thing that would rescue the community.

The residents of Nome organized a relay of sled dogs to cross over the Iditarod Trail to Anchorage. They needed to pick the right dogs to lead the teams. These dogs had to be very special, as they would have to give their all to push through the worst climate ever experienced in the world. This trip had also to be done in stages, with different groups of dogs, until they couldn't run anymore. The remaining two stages of the voyage were the hardest, and this was the key to making the journey. Gunnar Kaasen and his sled dog team were headed by an insignificant dog named Balto.

Contrary to Balto's status as a weak leader,

Gunnar believed this was the perfect dog because he was all heart. This white-on-black Siberian Husky boldly pushed through the gale-force winds and the blinding, raging blizzard. On February 2, 1925, Balto and the crew reached Nome just before sunrise.

The whole community was rescued after the serum was given. Balto and Kaasen were recognized as national heroes, and a big statue of Balto was built and is still visible in Central Park, New York, today.

The Cultural and Beliefs of American Indians

Does your family have a religion or a belief? Do you know what it is? If you don't know, ask Mom or Dad to explain it to you. Did you know that people take their religion or beliefs seriously? It's never a good thing to laugh at someone's beliefs. Below, we are going to have a look at what the Eskimo people believed in.

Traditional Inuit tribes believed in shamanism and animism, which involved spiritual healers, and meditating on these spirits. While many Inuit today practice Christianity, traditional Inuit spirituality still exists to a small degree in modern Inuit civilizations. Some Inuit have integrated, or brought together, indigenous beliefs with

Christian doctrine, which is called religious syncretism.

The cosmology or mythology of the Inuit people tells a story about the world and how the Eskimos play a part in it. In this religion, there isn't anyone who is in charge of the Inuit universe. There are no deities, or gods, that rule over their people. Nor are there sun or wind gods. There are no eternal punishments either, just as there is no punishment for kids or adults in their culture. Inuit mythology, rituals, and stigmas are frequently centered around the dangers of the cold Arctic environment.

The Inuit tribes are fearful about the future, and this sets the background for most of their early beliefs. There is always an evil spirit that hinders or kills and a healer or helper that will assist.

Iglulik Religion
The Inuit tribes have various beliefs, one being the Iglulik religion, where a spiritual healer known as angekku helped the Eskimos to release the marine animals. These animals are captured and hidden in the basement by a Sea woman called Takanaluk-arnaluk.

Netsilik Inuit
The Netsili Inuit religion, or Eskimos of the

Seal, is a religion that mainly guards against starvation in the winter months. In this religion, the Inuit use a lot of amulets or decorations made up of little pieces of jewelry that are believed to offer a defense against danger, evil, and disease. The tribe also believes that the tattoos inscribed on them will give them an option for where they can go in the afterlife.

Angakkuq

The Sea Lady, Nuliajuk, was referred to as 'the lubricous one.' She kept marine animals down in her basin, where she kept the qulliq– which means she kept animals in a basin where she held a lamp that burns seal fat.

If any of the tribe's people broke certain taboos or laws, the angakkuq (a healer and religious person the Inuit chose) was forced to go to her and plead for food. Nuliajuk was once an orphan girl who suffered abuse from her village, according to Netsilik's oral history.

Moon Man

Another cosmic creature from the Netsilik tribe, Moon Man, is called on, as he is kind to humankind and helps souls to enter the celestial realms.

The Caribou Inuit

This tribe's religion does not form a political

group, and the members have only occasional fellowship. However, they do share a way of life in the heartland and certain cultural similarities.

The Caribou believe that the soul is two-fold. The soul is connected to breathing, known as umaffia (place of life), and a child's individual soul is known as tarneq. The tarneq is viewed as being so frail that it requires the care of a name-soul of a dead relative. It was believed that the ancestor's physical presence in the body of the kid would lead to its gentler side with regard to its behavior, and this was often directed towards the boys.

To speak to fortunes or a form of a spirit guide, Qilaneq, a method of questioning a qila, was used by the Caribou angakkuit. The angakkuq set his glove down before raising his belt and staff to cover it. While inside the glove, the qila draws the staff to itself. Many such Alaskan Native groups use the qilaneq method, which is a process that offers a "yes" or "no" reply to questions asked.

Spirits and Creatures

To keep kids from walking to the coast by themselves, Inuit parents and elders scare the children by telling them the tale or legend known as Qallupilluit or Qalupalik. Qalupalik are aquatic creatures that resemble humans and have long hair, green skin, and long fingernails. They wear amautiit, the parka that Inuit women wear, which they use to kidnap infants and kids who defy their parents or stray off by themselves. The children are taken underwater, where they are raised by the creatures.

In order to prevent their kids from wandering off to the dangerous shore, parents today continue to tell their kids the Qalupalik story. Elders claim that when Qalupaliks are nearby, you can hear them humming because they have a characteristic humming sound.

There were other legends as well. Ahkiyyini is another creature that resembles a ghostly skeleton. The Inuit's description of Bigfoot or the Yeti story is known as Saumen Kar, also known by the names Tornit or Tuniit. This description might be a description of the Dorset tribe, who were rumored to be giants. There are also monsters called Tizheruk that resemble snakes.

Tales the Communities Would Tell
Stories were told as entertainment, or they referred to certain ceremonies they were taking part in. Below are a few fascinating tales.

Interesting Tales

The Inuit people, who live in the far North of the Americas, had a story. They spoke about Crow, who charmed them with tales of the clear skies and bright light when their sky was dark.

The crow flew South when they urged him to bring them bright light. When he came to a village, the crow transformed into a speck of dust that followed a little girl inside the chieftain's hut. He appeared in a child's ear and told her to play with the light orb sphere within a container in the hut before taking one outdoors.

Crow then returned to his original form, snatched up the light orb in his beak, and soared back toward the North. The crow dropped the light orb, and when it broke on the ground, it gave the Inuit people the light they desired.

The crow became elderly and worn out, so he rested for six months. Then once he collected his strength, he brought the light back to the Inuit people. As a result, there are six months of daylight and six months of darkness for the Inuit people, who also always treat the crow with kindness.

Initial Tears

This narrative, or story, describes the first

tears, which is another Inuit myth. In this story, a man is out in search of food to feed his wife and son. He spots a large herd of seals while out hunting by the water. He notices one in the distance that doesn't appear to see him, and he feels relieved.

"This one will feed the woman and children for several days," he thinks, and this makes the man quite pleased as he sees how fat and healthy the animal is. As he tries to creep up towards it, the seal suddenly swims away into the ocean. The man begins to cry water out of his eyes because he is so disappointed.

His pleas of sorrow are heard by a woman and son, who run to help him. They also begin to cry when he tells them about the seal. After this event, the man and son receive the method in a vision of how to catch seals by using sinew skins to make traps.

Why the Opossum Hasn't Got Fur on Its Tail

Many animals use their long, bushy tails to wave around, brush off insects, and keep themselves warm in winter. But other animals— especially Rabbit, who was envious of these animals with wonderful tails, began to fight with those with large tails.

Opossum once had a gorgeous, bushy tail that he often flailed up and showed off in front of the animals. So, Rabbit planned to trick Opossum and damage his pride.

Rabbit created a plan that would affect the dance they had all planned for that night. Rabbit asked Cricket to pretend to comb Opossum's hair and wrap it with a scarlet cord. Opossum was put to sleep by the combining, and his tail was still wrapped up when he awoke.

As Opossum danced in front of all the other animals, he freed his tail from the wrap during the dance, exclaiming how lovely his tail was. His tail was bare as Cricket had removed every hair while he was asleep, and the other animals mocked and made fun of him. Opossum was so startled when he saw his hairless tail that he collapsed in horror. This was such a traumatic experience that nowadays, opossums always collapse when they look at their tails.

CHAPTER 3
LIFE OF NATIVE AMERICANS

American Indian communities in the North created dwellings that were simple to erect, dismantle, and move elsewhere. Most of these tribal groups kept changing locations or places to stay because they were following the herds of bison they were hunting.

There were certain Native dwellings that looked like leather tents, and their design changed with the weather. Yet, many families enjoyed living together in one big home. Whereas only a small number of people would live in tiny lodgings.

The American tribes in the Great Plains made tepees from buffalo skin. Some tribes used a lot of different materials when creating a dwelling. For instance, they would use nearby young trees with flexible growth, leaves, and animal fur in their structure.

Most tribes used grasses and other materials to create more layers to the teepee to create insulation in the winter months. A fire was also built in the middle of the teepee to keep the family warm.

The underneath hide covering was lifted during the hotter months to let cool air circulate in the living space. Have you ever gone camping with your family? It's fun to cook your food outdoors and have a few smores over an open fire.

Two Little Crow Members, 1895

Do you love to have long walks, swim in the river, or lie under the stars at night to get close to nature? Well, this is how the American Indians lived! They would pack up after a while and move their tents elsewhere.

The Choctaw tribe created their dwelling out

of wooden planks that were bound together with a flexible cane or wood band, and this construction is known as a wigwam dwelling. It was round or dome-shaped and was covered with grass or leaves. These dwellings were often seen in several areas of America.

The only opening to a wigwam dwelling was a little door, and the wood walls were completely covered with mud for further insolation. There were certain cultures that created underground structures to store food in, and they were also covered in layers of organic material.

The Pueblo Indians of Southwest America constructed their homes with sun-dried bricks made from clay. The community also used stone, wood, and adobe - which is similar to cement. There were tribes that lived in Pueblos, and these tribes had a long history of farming.

Historically, we refer to all Pueblo people—past and present—as 'Pueblo people' or 'Pueblo Indians.' This title also refers to those who lived in the distant past, as they were the Pueblo ancestors. The ancient Pueblo Indians are frequently referred to as the 'ancestral Pueblo.' Another term used is the Anasazi people, and they come from the first Pueblo inhabitants. The Spanish term 'pueblo' means 'village' or 'town.' I wonder if the Spanish used this term to describe the impressive villages the tribes created.

The Southwestern region, where the tribes settled, is the only area where four states corner each other in the U.S. The cornered states are made up of Colorado, Utah, Arizona, and New Mexico.

The Mesa Verde area is home to the tribe's distant past and thousands of exciting ancient finds. The houses they built were originally one story tall and had flat roofs, but some grew a lot bigger.

Kivas is a name used to describe an area or a building in which meetings and ceremonies occurred. Some Kivas were placed in towns, while others became very large. They were built on the outskirts of the town. In the later stages, houses were built into cliffs, and some dwellings grew to four stories high. We will investigate more about this era a bit later on when we read about 'The Mesa Verde.'

A Rust Color Statue

Baths, Kitchens, and Hygiene

In the early days, Native Americans didn't have bathrooms and kitchens in their homes, as we do. The majority of American tribes had free baths in rivers and streams, much like the Wampanoag group tribes did.

This group of people often bathed together in the rivers, and this event came naturally to them. This dynamic group settled in Eastern Rhode Island and modern-day Massachusetts.

The Wampanoag people have been a tribe

for more than 12,000 years, and they are sometimes known as 'the People of the first light.' These creative people are known for their exquisite artistic products; today, the Wampanoag still makes beautiful baskets, wood carvings, and beaded items.

These are a diverse group of indigenous people that included many more tribes, communities, and cultures than there are today. The ancient Indians were extremely hygienic and took three daily baths a day, and they washed their body's very well.

A Sweat Lodge

A sweat lodge was another way to "bathe" in winter, and it was a spiritual experience for the tribal people. The building was a dome-shaped structure, and it was created out of organic materials. When tribal groups discussed a sweat lodge, they spoke about a ritual that took place inside the building.

This ritual involved cleansing the body, mind, and soul at a religious or spiritual level. This ritual was also used to help with prayer - often directed towards healing and organized under the direction of a leader. The societies where it was traditionally practiced held it in high regard as being ancient, sacred, and a greatly treasured experience.

Every element of their ceremonies was profoundly infused with spiritual meaning. In the North American Indigenous custom, the lodges were built with willow bark that was bowed and set into the ground in a circular shape. This building was also covered with blankets, which were usually animal skins.

Hot basalt stones were positioned in the center of the room and covered in water and therapeutic herbs. These stones held the heat that filled the steam house. The tribes believed that the ghosts or spirits of all their ancestors stayed in the stones. Whenever water was splashed on these stones, the ancestors would emerge from the stones after being awakened by the fire's intense heat.

The ancestors would then enter the Native American's body as they emerged from the stone. This spiritual process was said to expel any pain felt by the tribe members. Native tribes also believe that ancestor ghosts left some of their wisdom when departing from the stones. In fact, today, believers that partake in sweat lodge rituals evangelize about the clarity of mind and vigor of body, and spiritual renewal they experienced in the sweat lodge.

American Indians Created Their Own Cleaning Products

The Native Americans created their own hair shampoo in those days from smashed young yucca plant roots that were soaked in water. The tribe would also peel or slice up the yucca root and then rub it in the small of their hand with water to produce suds that were massaged into their scalp and hair. Why don't you try and make your own organic shampoo and soap? Don't forget to ask a parent to help you!

Did you know that the tribes' believed Europeans were disgusting because they carried handkerchiefs filled with their own phlegm, or boogers, around with them? Usually, the bathroom "business" was done in an area that was practical and near enough to their teepees.

Native Americans also dug latrines (toilets) far enough from teepees or dwellings and their clean water sources to avoid diseases. Latrines would, however, be situated even closer to their dwellings during the worst weather. This wasn't a problem because in winter, everything froze, and nothing ever smelt bad.

Almost all of the materials used by the various tribes were biodegradable or would naturally break down because they were made from natural products. Overall, people from the Indian settlements were far cleaner than those who lived in European cities.

Native Indians also made their own toothbrushes with a stick called a chewstick. These chew sticks had two sides; one side was sharpened to function as a toothpick, whereas the other end was flattened and broken up on a rock and used for brushing and polishing teeth.

When mom or dad buys the groceries, they often choose a certain brand of toothpaste. Well, the Native Indians did something similar, as they had their preferences. They chose from a selection of natural products they liked. Here are a few: fresh herbs, salt, and leaves were rubbed on their teeth to freshen their breath.

Cucacua plants were also used, as they made a product similar to toothpaste with it. Some used pine needles as sandpaper to clear plaque from their teeth, and it also helped to freshen their breath. Neither the Pilgrims nor the Native Americans had the same level of oral health as we do now. Aren't you happy about that?

Ways of Cooking Different Dishes

Without ovens, the Indians hardly baked anything, but they used shallow pots positioned right over hot coals outdoors. They had enough animal fat and could extract oil from foods such as nuts and sunflower seeds, but they didn't like to use too much oil and didn't fry anything.

In parts of Northeastern Carolina, Indians prepared a wide range of foods in four basic ways: raw, stewed, broiled, and dried. When the food became dry, with or without the use of fire, it was restored or rehydrated with water.

The majority of the nuts and fruit eaten by the Indians were raw. Moreover, they ate pieces of raw pumpkin and squash and chewed on raw roots called okeepenauk, which most people would find difficult to stomach.

American Bison

Making Tools and Hunting and Farming

Some tribes did relocate, and they settled in one area for a long time. They didn't have the means to hunt marine mammals, which the Inuit hunted at the time. Compared to the Inuit skin boats, the birch bark canoes that the American Indians used were much less suited for survival in open water. So, they only used their boats for lake and river fishing.

The American Indians didn't know how to make tools such as harpoons either, which had removable heads for killing marine life. Yet the Indian Americans were brilliant farmers and gatherers, and land hunters.

The arrival of the Europeans also meant numerous weapons (e.g., guns) became available. Horses were also brought back into hunting the bison on the Great open Plains. Horticulture, or growing food crops, became a full-time lifestyle for these hunters and gatherers.

Hunting and gathering have always played a big role in American Indian communities. Native tribes also used natural materials, such as rock, twine, bark, oyster shell, clay, and plant material, to make their tools and weapons. A Ute lithic tribe's tool was recently found and is on show at Florissant Fossil Beds National Monument.

The Ute lithi people were similar to many

other tribes, who crafted their tools by grinding stones. They also made bowls and weaponry, such as arrows and bows, knives, and shields from natural resources.

Ceremonial and Hunting Ground

The tribes had traditional hunting grounds, and these included the present-day states of Wyoming, Arizona, Oklahoma, and New Mexico, in addition to their ancestral homeland in Colorado and Utah. The tribes also had holy places that were visited on a seasonal basis outside of their territory.

There were eleven historical Ute groups or bands. Several Ute bands were culturally impacted by the Puebloan tribes and other nearby Native American tribes since they often traded. Yes, these communities would still come together for rituals and trading, even though they often hunted and gathered in their own family groups.

Native American Dogs

Native American dogs surprised nineteenth-century explorers and naturalists when they first saw them, as they looked just like wolves. Large and powerful animals, and instead of them barking, the creatures howled.

In fact, the wolf-like animals, Audubon

observed, were genetically different from those in Europe. The researchers have tested dog bones that were found to be buried. They discovered that these canines were 'precontact dogs,' meaning that these dogs were buried near or with humans, and they were closely linked to 9000-year-old canines from Russia's Zhokhov Island, which were located thousands of kilometers North of the Siberian peninsula.

The team created and calculated a 'molecular clock,' which means they found two groups of dogs that shared an early ancestor that was linked to 16,000 years ago. They created a 'roughly - constant' DNA. The origin of these dogs remains unknown, but it may have occurred around the specified period.

It is likely that the American Natives at the time used these dogs to help hunt (Grimm, 2018). Pets are wonderful when they are part of the family and often give a person a lot of love. Do you have pets at home? What type of pets are they?

Head Pieces and Headdress

Did you know that many tribes covered their heads with bird feathers? A feathered headpiece that is connected to the full upper portion of a leather headband is known as a Native headdress. Beadwork or genuine leather can be used to decorate the headband.

Typically, the feathers on the headdress come from a dead bird that is indigenous to the region - where the tribe makes the headdress. Depending on how the creative person or artist wants the headdress to look, the feathers can be arranged in a variety of ways and are fixed together with leather pieces, thread, or sinew.

The Sioux are thought to have been the first tribes to wear headpieces made of feathers. The Native Americans from North America saw a headdress as a well-known symbol of courage and strength.

A headdress was important since it showed certain members of the tribe, they were brave, and they had influence or fame within a tribe. Headdresses were not created in a day; they needed time, and the length of time taken depended on how valuable and precious the headdress was to that person.

Certain feathers or designs meant different things, and they told a story. Wearing one of these stunning works of art is not just an honor; it also adds to the meaning of the headdress.

Both genders were allowed to wear a headdress; the main distinction was that men chose a battle bonnet, while women preferred the beaded headband look because it was pretty and feminine.

Don't you think it would be awesome to wear a headpiece now that you know what it means? Well, the tribe feels strongly that no one else should wear a headpiece that hasn't worked hard enough to earn it.

Only prominent community members, such as the chief and certain warriors, could wear a very large headdress, as it showed the bravery of that person. It's actually considered to be disrespectful to those who have earned their headpiece when other people wear it. Most activists find it extremely offensive to the meaning and the worth of the headpiece. When considering what outfit to wear for Halloween, for instance, avoid wearing American Indian headpieces.

The Aboriginal Americans of Canada and the United States also used certain headdresses during the war. Today, you would probably see a headdress being worn during a pow-wow, which is a traditional wedding ceremony, or other similar events.

Turning Eagle's Headpiece, a Member of the Sioux Tribe, 1898

Lives Were Dictated by the Seasons

The lives of the American Indians were dictated by the seasons. These seasons decide on the types of food that Native Americans ate, what clothes they wore, and what kind of shelters they used. So, the seasons affected all their choices.

The tribes hunted birds and other animals in winter and continued to live off the food they preserved or saved from the previous fall. In order to conserve and store food for the winter, they gathered their crops and went hunting in the fall.

Native People used a lot of natural resources in many different ways. The main responsibilities of the men in the Native Indian tribes were to Hunt, fish, and protect the community. The community would go out and gather or forage wild edibles from the area around them in the warmer months, and that was often berries, roots, nuts, and herbs.

They were dressed in deerskin, which is animal skin. Most tribes made clothing out of animal skins, plant matter, and furs. Particularly well-liked skins and furs were that of the buffalo and the rabbit. Simple skirts were worn by tropical Indian tribes. Then there were several tribes that wore nothing at all except a few pieces of leather.

Every winter, men from many tribes would band or group together and go out on hunting trips. If they caught a large animal, it would be shared among them all. Their diet consisted of venison or deer meat, and this was combined with an agrarian diet—which meant it was made up of large amounts of grass seeds, such as natural grains or planted wheat, lentils, barley, and maize.

European settlers exposed the Choctaw to farming crops, like beans and corn, over the course of many years. Due to the start of agriculture, they created different food-based meals in their culture and traditions. Their movement and exchange of ideas further influenced this change.

The aIti Fabvssa newspaper claimed that the Choctaw people eventually adopted agriculture around the year 1000 AD, and these tribes were regarded as the best agricultural producers among the various Southeastern Tribes" (Biskinik Newspaper, 2022).

The Powhatan Indian tribes were also made up of good farmers who would work fields of about 100 acres in size or length. The women were in charge of maintaining the fields, and they used many different crafted tools and objects, such as bone and deer antlers. The Powhatan tribes grew sunflowers, beans, corn, squash, and pumpkins.

The women were also responsible for preparing meals from the crops planted and the food gathered. They created wonderful dishes such as corn cakes and hominy from the major crop that was produced, which was maize.

Marriage and Family Life

In certain Indian tribes, relatives chose their children's wives or husbands for them. Tribal people typically married early, between the ages of 13 and 20. Often the Indian cultures allowed men to have multiple wives.

The Iroquois Group was different from the majority of tribes. These tribal people were made up of five smaller tribes, and they lived in a matrilineal society - meaning that the wife or woman was seen to be the head of the home. The five groups that made up the Iroquois group were: Onondaga, Mohawk, Oneida, Seneca, and Cayuga tribes.

In contrast to the custom, whenever an Iroquois man married an Iroquois woman, he would join her and her family. These tribes from the East would live as a hundred or more people in longhouses that were mostly built from bark.

These tribal Indians frequently stayed with their extended families, and this was what I explained to be a clan. A clan is a collection of relatives who share a common ancestor. Wouldn't it be wonderful to live with your cousins, whom you miss so much?

In summer months, these tribes would move closer to a water source, such as a river or a lake, and stay in wigwam dwellings. Frequently, after the death of a husband, the widow would move in with a brother of her late husband's family.

Due to the high death rate of infants and young children within the Indian tribe at the time, the majority of households were small. Like many Native Americans, Choctaw moms carried their infants on their backs in cradleboards.

A boy's strength and bravery were often put to the test as they grew older. Most of the tribal boys went to ceremonies and performed rituals. They also went for long periods, where they would live off the land or go hunting for their survival in the bush. Tribal people spent a lot of their time defending and fending off other tribes until the Europeans arrived.

Children in the community may have had a similar childhood to what you have been having. They played with one another, attended school, and assisted with household chores. They also have toys and games to play with; one toy was called a Toli or a stickball game.

This was a favorite activity for both adolescent boys and grown men. Girls from the Choctaw tribe loved playing a lot of guessing games, and they also played with their beaded dolls. Sports included foot races, football, and swimming, and these sports were especially popular among Choctaw children.

They also loved the game, Chunky. This was when a disc-shaped object was rolled over the ground, and spears were thrown toward it in an effort to land them as near to the halted object as possible. I have a few more of these activities that we will investigate in detail further in the book.

Many young Choctaw people enjoyed hunting and fishing with their fathers. Indian children would, however, have more responsibilities and less time for play than I think you may do.

The Language That Was Spoken

Some tribes spoke rhythmic languages like the Choctaw, and this was almost the same as Chickasaw. Chickasaw is derived from the Muskogean language group. Today, these tribes often stay in Alabama, Seminole, Koasati, Mvskoke, Hitchiti, and Mikasuki.

The two basic languages can actually communicate quite well with one another. Come on, let's try and learn a couple of simple Choctaw words—Start with "yakoke" (pronounced yah-koh-keh) means "thank you," and "halito" (pronounced hah-lih-toh) is a kind greeting.

The Cultural and Beliefs of American Indians

The ethnic groups within the United States have the highest cultural differences to date. These tribes were all living on the same continent for thousands of years. Yet, the American Native communities have very different family structures, cultural backgrounds and religious traditions, value systems, languages, and clothing styles.

The racial differences between American Indians and Alaska Natives are similar to that of the European people. However, their language and cultural differences are far different from one another.

The American Indians tend to emphasize values of cosmic identity - which is harmony between the person and the tribe; the tribe and the land; and harmony between the land as well as the spirit of the universe or cosmos.

A sense of stability and balance is needed, with the regularity of nature as the source of its existence. So, it was important for them to achieve balance when searching for harmony. This cycle shows that their eternity means: to have life in reality, which moves into space or a sphere of all things and respects all things.

The tribal culture puts a high focus on harmony or as stated before, the tribe living together with nature. Other factors are the ability to endure pain and the respect for others in the tribe. Then to have the conviction that people are essentially good and deserving of respect for their choices. Below are a few major concepts of their religion.

- The most primitive of the tribes in North America had, by the time Europeans arrived, evolved, or developed ideas into their religious systems that included cosmologies—creation myths that were passed down from one generation to the next and explained how those societies had come into being.
- The majority of these tribes revered or worshiped an all-knowing, all-powerful Creator known as the "Master Spirit." They related to this spirit as a 'Being,' that took on a variety of forms as well as both genders (male and female).
- They also worshiped and tried to please and put up with several lesser-known supernatural 'Beings,' including a male violent supernatural 'Being' who brought

destruction, misery, and death.
- The majority of tribal members believed in the human soul and an afterlife that is characterized by an abundance of good things. This sphere makes life on earth feel secure, for instance, ideas of immortality and a life of eternity that follows it.
- Each tribe in North America had its own set of religious rituals that were focused on. Ultimately, they all boiled down to the same goal, as all other cultures: using the supernatural to influence the natural as well as the social environment.
- Individual tribal people tried to 'woo' or satisfy powerful spiritual entities with personal prayers or sacrifices or expensive objects that were collected in raids or products they had, such as furs, animals, tobacco, food products, etc.

Divine Help and Support in Everyday Matters

When entire towns wanted to seek divine help and support to ensure a successful hunt or a good harvest, or victory in warfare, they called upon Shaman priests, and in a few tribes, they had priestesses. The tribe believed these priests or priestesses had supernatural powers, as they received visions.

This would also include manipulating the weather, which was of fundamental importance to the entire tribe. Shamans also had the unusual ability to read dreams and change the course of the future, cure different types of diseases, or curse others with witchcraft.

Creation Tale

Several stories were kept for particular seasons or evenings of the year because they were considered sacred or spiritual. The tales still serve to protect the tribal people, as well as their legacy and customs. These tales and stories often served as the inspiration for a tribe's unique rituals and celebrations.

Traditional tribes, societies, or cultures believed in a creation tale, which is similarly described in a book of the Bible called Genesis. They describe a revered Creator or God, and they feared a cunning lesser god such as Lucifer and looked forward to their soul's finding eternity.

They also worshiped a god with prayers and offerings, and a highly educated priesthood supported their society during difficult times. The majority of early modern Europeans worried about witches and wondered what their dreams meant.

The fact of the matter is that Native Americans did not make a distinction between the natural and the paranormal. Indian Americans saw the 'spiritual' and 'material' as having no boundaries and together or an interconnected reality.

They believed in 'guardian spirits,' and a wide variety of 'supernatural Beings' that gave their "natural life" power over to people. They also believe they are one with the animals, plants, and humans, allowing them to share in divinity (supernatural power).

For instance, a totem animal was the story of a person's life, a generational progression, or a tribe's spiritual representation in Native American culture. In the Native Indian culture, a totem animal serves as a 'guiding spirit' for the rest of a person's life or, rather, the lifetime of a family (Wikipedia, 2022). Below are some tales that were told in the tribal communities.

The Mist Maiden

The Woman of the Mist tale is probably the most significant of the many tales surrounding the Falls. The Ongiaras Tribe stayed close to a cascade of water that would later be called Niagara Falls.

The tribe chose to sacrifice the most

attractive young woman in their community to the falls since they had unexpectedly fallen on hard times, and many of their members were dying in strange ways.

The young woman entered a white colored, birch canoe while she herself was dressed in a white doeskin gown, and there were flowers in her hair. She was the daughter of the chief, and it was agreed that if they wanted a favor, they would need to sacrifice this beautiful maiden.

As the maiden plunged to her death over the Falls, the chief was overcome with grief, and he decided he couldn't live without his daughter, so he jumped after her. The thunder god Hinum, who stayed beneath the falls, was touched by the act, so he took the young woman in his arms and brought her back to his cave, where he lived with his two sons. One of the sons decided to marry the maiden.

Her newly married husband told her that a huge snake was harming her people. The girl forewarned her tribe 'in spirit', and the tribe found the snake and fatally wounded it. After that incident, the Horseshoe Falls were created.

Fire

The Cherokee tribe that once lived in what is now the Alabama area created tales about the beginnings of fire. According to mythology, the bear was the first to possess fire, and he took it along with him for his family everywhere they went.

They came across a lot of wonderful acorns one day in the forest, so the bear decided to build a fire at the very edge of a line of trees. While they munched on the roasted nuts, they chatted and continued to move further away from the fire until they could no longer hear it calling to them.

A man that was passing by heard the plea of the fire as it cried, "feed me, feed me!" He gave it some wood and twigs to help it survive. Bear eventually came back, and the fire was upset with him; he chased Bear away with his harsh light. From that day, fire allowed man to become the new owner of fire, which made the man very happy.

CHAPTER 4
THREE FAMOUS NATIVE AMERICANS

Learning from different cultures and famous people from the past creates a fantastic opportunity as it teaches us how to control our emotions and show bravery in the face of fear.

Broadly exploring various cultures and people gives us new insights that might help others and ourselves cope with changes and overcome turbulent times.

Native People, for instance, had to overcome a lot of hardship. Their lessons in life show us how to be emotionally healthy, strong, loyal, and peace-loving,to fight for our freedom, and never give up. We need to try our best in life and hold onto good teachings and values, so we can show the rest of the world how to act.

Pocahontas
The story of a young American Native

woman called Pocahontas (Seong Yujin), and Captain John Smith (Lee Jeong-gu) landed up being a Disney animated movie. You all know the movie Pocahontas, don't you? Well, let me refresh your memory. The movie portrays Pocahontas as a beautiful woman and the daughter of the chief.

John Smith described her in his novel to be a stunning Native girl and the daughter of a Chief who saved him, an English explorer, from being put to death by her father.

Pocahontas left her people and joined the English because there was love at first sight. She traveled to a new Country with other settlers to start a new life. I think you remember it now (Stebbins, 2017)!

Well, the actual life story of Pocahontas was far different from how Smith or the popular culture portrayed it to be. Let's investigate the sad tale of Pocahontas. In the early 1600s, there were many dangers that the tribes close to Werowocomoco had to endure.

When the English colonists arrived in the area, they stole women and children, as many of their own families had been attacked and killed or stolen by tribal people.

Pocahontas name was actually Amonute, but

she was known as Matoaka. She was just 15 or 16 years old at the time when the risk of kidnapping became a real threat. Regrettably, Pocahontas was abducted, and her first child was left behind in the confusion. The people that kidnapped her fought with the tribe, and her husband, Kocoum, who she had recently married, was killed.

Captain Samuel Argall, who headed the English colonists, set out in the hope that he could capture the chief's daughter, and this would stop the Native American tribes from attacking them. During the conflict of 1613, Pocahontas was taken prisoner and held for ransom by English colonists in the prisons, where she was treated very badly.

Later, Argall warned the chief that if he didn't stop his attacks on the Europeans, he was going to put a complete end to them all. Then Samuel Argall presented the chief with a copper pot and stated that he had swapped it for his daughter, Pocahontas. It was clear how little regard people had for human life on both sides in those days.

Pocahontas was persuaded to become a Christian while she was a captive, and she was baptized and given the name Rebecca. She was about 17 or 18 years old at the time when she apparently married the owner of a tobacco plantation called John Rolfe in April 1614. Shortly after, she gave birth to their son, Thomas, in January 1615 (Wikipedia Contributors, 2018).

Pocahontas was taken to England as a political sign of peace and harmony between English colonists and Native American tribes. According to Mattachanna's reports, she became aware that she was being used for their own profit against her tribes (Stebbins, 2017).

Pocahontas yearned to go back to her father and young Kocoum. Pocahontas met John Smith in England, and she conveyed her emotions to him. She explained how the colonists had treated her when she was captured and that she was not prepared to betray the Powhatan people anymore.

Pocahontas was scheduled to arrive back at her house in the spring of 1617. According to Mattachanna's stories, Pocahontas was healthy and in good shape at the time. Yet soon after eating supper with John Rolfe and Argall, Pocahontas vomited up her food and fell over dead (Stebbins, 2017).

She barely reached the age of 21 when she died. Despite the fact that her family wanted her remains to be buried on the tribal grounds, Rolfe and Argall transported her body to Gravesend, England, so that she could be buried at a chapel.

After Mattachanna, her father, learned that his daughter had passed away, he was devastated by the news. Within a year of Pocahontas's death, the chief apparently also died from grief (Wikipedia Contributors, 2018).

A Chiricahua Apache Girl

Sacagawea

Another life story about a wonderful, brave

young woman. Sacagawea was born in either 1788 or 1789 and was a Native American Shoshone tribal woman. She traveled and translated for the Lewis and Clark expedition, which took place from 1804 to 1806. The expedition, also known as the 'Corps of Discovery,' made its way from the Northern plains to the Pacific Ocean and then back via the Rocky Mountains.

All these early discoveries helped us to create roads and to learn about the geography, flora (plants), and fauna (animals) of the region, as well as how the Louisiana Purchase might have been used for financial benefit.

Sacagawea's abilities as a translator and her in-depth understanding of the treacherous or hidden dangers of the terrain and how to live in the wild become priceless to everyone. For instance, she became vital to the cause because of her positive personality and the influence she had on the expedition crew and all the Native Americans they came across who would have been otherwise hostile. Amazingly, Sacagawea took her infant child along with her on the expedition.

Sacagawea led a short but eventful life throughout the American West, and she is arguably the most recognized and honored

American Native woman in the country. There are many statues and monuments that are dedicated to her work and bravery today.

As a child, Sacagawea lived in the Salmon River area of what is now Idaho, and it is bordered by the Rocky Mountains. She was also a part of the Lemhi band of Native Americans, and they were called the Shoshone tribe.

The Shoshone tribe was a rival of the armed Hidatsa tribe, who abducted Sacagawea in 1800 while they were out hunting buffalos. The name Sacagawea is actually a Hidatsa term for 'bird woman.' The word 'Sacaga' means woman, and 'wea' means bird. Her real name was Sacajawea, which meant 'boat-pusher.' The kidnappers took her to the Hidatsa-Mandan, to one of the members of the Mandan tribe, not far from what is now known as Bismarck, North Dakota.

Toussaint Charbonneau, a French-Canadian fur merchant, who had spent so much time dealing with Native People, eventually accepted some of their customs, such as polygamy. Polygamy meant having many wives at once, and if you wanted to get a divorce, a man would say in front of everyone that he had "thrown away his woman"; most often, the men would also beat on a drum. All the women had to do to get a divorce or get rid of her spouse was take everything she owned back to her parent's tepee.

Anyway, Sacagawea was later obtained by Toussaint Charbonneau in a gambling payment. Sacagawea was pregnant at the time of her exchange. However, if a woman became a possession from a raid, they could exchange or sell their wives, as in the case of Sacagawea.

Yet, President Thomas Jefferson, at the time, expected to learn a lot from his planned exploration of this passageway that he had heard so much about. He wanted the team to map the area and evaluate the topography–the study of where the rivers, mountains, grasslands are, etc. They needed to learn about the different Native American tribes and gather natural samples. He asked Meriwether Lewis, his secretary, to lead the Corps of Discovery. Lewis, 29, agreed and asked William Clark, a 33-year-old friend, and retired military superior, to serve as his co-captain.

Toussaint Charbonneau and his wife Sacagawea were also asked to join the exploration because they had knowledge about the Native tribes and the area. On November 2, 1804, when Sacagawea was about six months pregnant, Lewis and Clark and their men arrived at the Hidatsa-Mandan village.

This was well after a year of intense preparation for the initial journey. The majority of the Corps members were English speakers, except Francois Labiche, who could also speak French. Sacagawea spoke Shoshone and Hidatsa, while Charbonneau spoke French and Hidatsa (two very different languages).

On February 11, 1805, Sacagawea gave birth to her son Jean-Baptiste Charbonneau also known as Baptiste. By April 7, along with the other thirty-one Corps members, Sacagawea, the infant, and Charbonneau departed for the West.

Some 60 miles Northwest of modern-day Bismarck, North Dakota. They realized the potential benefit of having the language skills that Sacagawea spoke. At this point, Lewis and Clark also realized that they had to buy horses from the Shoshone tribe. They needed horses to carry their supplies through the treacherous Bitterroot Mountains and carry them toward the ocean.

A near-tragic event that happened within a month of the journey brought Sacagawea special honor. Sacagawea had the foresight to gather important documents, books, navigational aids, medicines, as well as other supplies that would have otherwise vanished when the sailing boat hit the squall. The squall is a gusting wind that only lasts a few seconds; it's fast and causes a dramatic rise in wind speed. It often happens along with stormy weather, heavy snowfall, or rain showers. Anyway, let me carry on–A few days later, Lewis and Clark celebrated Sacagawea by giving her the name of a Missouri River tributary. After that, Sacagawea and Baptiste accompanied Clark by pacing the shore to look for any hazards in the river that may harm the boats. Clark grew especially close to Sacagawea.

Sacagawea also greatly helped the expedition when she explained to the Shoshone people, they met that they needed to buy horses. Chief Cameahwait was really the Shoshone tribe's chief, and Sacagawea was shocked and overjoyed to realize that he was also her brother. They ended up having a beautiful, emotional reunion together.

Sacagawea used her knowledge as a naturalist to the benefit of the expedition. She was able to recognize both medicinal and edible plants, such as berries and roots. Clark referred to Sacagawea as his 'pilot' because her skill, as well as her knowledge about the Shoshone paths, were phenomenal.

She assisted in directing the group through

difficult areas, and one, in particular, was the mountain pass towards the Yellowstone River. The pass is now known as the 'Bozeman Pass,' which is located in Montana. In addition, the presence of a Native American woman and her baby helped a lot, as some tribespeople had never seen a European face before.

Sacagawea's presence made the entire corps appear less threatening and more friendly to the Native Americans. Sacagawea and her husband and kid had endured a variety of hardships such as sickness, severe storms, extreme heat, lack of food, mosquito swarms, and a lot more - as they traveled to the Pacific and returned with the rest of the expedition.

Three years later, Sacagawea, her husband, and her son traveled to St. Louis in the fall of 1809. The little family decided to take up an offer to allow Clark to educate Baptiste in exchange for the family farm. But the farming didn't work out, and in April 1811, Sacagawea and Toussaint traveled to join a fur-trading operation, leaving Baptiste in St. Louis with Clark, who was now his godfather.

Sacagawea fell pregnant again, but this time she had a baby girl. After Sacagawea's baby girl, Lizette, in August 1812, her health deteriorated quickly. She developed a severe case of what is thought to be typhoid fever. On December 22, 1812, at the age of twenty-five, Sacagawea died in Fort Manuel.

Within the year, Clark was appointed Baptiste and Lizette's legal guardian. Lisette's life is largely unknown, although Baptiste traveled throughout Europe and held a variety of occupations in the American West until passing away in 1866 (Wikipedia Contributors, 2019a).

Sitting Bull

Sitting Bull was born in South Dakota, and he was a member of the Lakota Sioux tribe. His folks referred to the place where he had been born as 'Many-Caches.' His father's name was Jumping Bull, and he was known as a fearsome warrior. His father gave him the nickname 'Slow' as he took time to act and acted with extreme caution.

In the Sioux tribe, 'Slow' had a regular childhood. He gained knowledge of horseback riding, bow hunting, and buffalo hunting. He envisioned himself as a great fighter one day in the future. 'Slow' shot his first buffalo at the age of ten.

This youngster then joined his first real battle party at the age of 14. During the events, he valiantly attacked a warrior in the conflict with the Crow tribe, taking him down. In recognition of his bravery, his father named him Sitting Bull once the group arrived back at camp.

The Europeans started to penetrate the tribal territory, and each year, they increased in number. Sitting Bull eventually rose to fame among his people and earned a reputation for his bravery. He wanted harmony with the white people, but they refused to leave his territory.

Sitting Bull started to use force and violence against Americans in 1863. He tried to frighten them away, but they kept coming back. He aided in Red Cloud's 1868 campaign against many local American forts.

Sitting Bull disagreed with Red Cloud when he signed a treaty with the new settlers, and he wouldn't approve any agreements that risked his land being taken away. By 1869, Sitting Bull was regarded as the Highest Chief of the Sioux tribe.

Gold had been discovered in 1874 in the Black Hills of South Dakota. The Europeans that were forming the new republic wanted access to the gold and didn't want tribal intervention.

The Sioux tribe was ordered to move to the

Sioux Reservation. Sitting Bull declined the offer. He believed that reservations functioned similarly to jail, and he did not want to be caged and locked up in a corral. His tribe had always lived as free people, and he was not going to allow the settlers to change it.

Sitting Bull established a war camp when American forces started to hunt down Lakota tribal people who stayed outside the reserve. Together with numerous other Native Indians from other tribes, such as the Cheyenne and the Arapaho tribes. His camp expanded rapidly, housing possibly an addition of 10,000 people that had joined as a force to be reckoned with.

Within his tribe, Sitting Bull was also revered as a holy figure. After engaging in a Sun Dance ceremony, he experienced a vision. He saw American soldiers falling like grasshoppers out of the sky. He claimed that his people would triumph in a vital fight that was about to occur.

The Native battle camp was fought not long after Sitting Bull's vision. On June 25, 1876, Colonel George Custer of the American Army was attacked. George Custer, however, was unaware of the magnitude of the army that Sitting Bull had accumulated.

Colonel George Custer and many other

members of his army were killed when the Indians completely defeated them. This conflict united Native Indians against the US Army and is regarded as one of the Native Tribes' greatest wins.

Even though the American Indians had won the Battle of Little Bighorn easily, more American troops quickly arrived in South Dakota. Sitting Bull was eventually forced to flee to Canada after his army dispersed or split up.

Sitting Bull decided to come back and surrender to the Americans in 1881. He decided he would have to live on the reservation after all. In 1890 the police feared that Sitting Bull would leave the reservation and join a sect known as the Ghost Dancers in a rally.

So, the police went to arrest Sitting Bull, but the police and Sitting Bull's followers landed in a shootout. Unfortunately, during the struggle, Sitting Bull was killed. This brave tribal man was courageous, and he stood for the freedom of his people.

When stories emerged about Sitting Bull as a powerful leader who aided in the maintenance of his people's traditional ways of life and the mistreatment, they all endured, it led to a change in how people currently treat the

American tribes (Wikipedia Contributors, 2019b).

CHAPTER 5
NATIVE AMERICAN ARTS & CRAFTS

Native American crafts that were created thousands of years ago are being used in tribal creative methods and technologies nowadays. Are you artistic, or do you have a family that is? Do you like to create beautiful things with your hands? Let's have a look at which Native American tribes were skilled with their hands in weaving and beading methods and who designed pottery items.

In this chapter, we will investigate tribes that produced these beautiful works of art and their distinctive styles.

Pottery

Pottery found in areas such as the Southwestern parts of America dates back to 4,000 BCE, although no one is quite sure where all these pieces came from.

The pottery that has been found on the American continent was designed and made by a variety of different tribal groups. Today it's easier to directly link a Native American tribe to their artwork.

What do you think the Native American pottery looked like? Do you think it was a basic brown color and roughly recognizable pieces made from a clay medium? Yes, you're right, somewhere! However, a lot was manufactured from earthenware clay and was well-shaped and rounded at the bottom. The pottery pieces also had a variety of colors, and this was achieved by using different soils. They also used the water from plants that were soaked when mixing the clay or when decorating pots with natural tools.

The tribes we are going to discuss were true artists, and they created beautiful pottery pieces. These tribes were the Iroquois, Pueblo, Shoshone, Cherokee, and Cheyenne tribes. Each of these tribes has put a lot of pride into their work and has shown distinctive qualities in their craftsmanship.

Certain tribes start by making clay coils, like you may have made with playdough - when rolling the clay between your hands and creating a long worm or snake. The Native tribes rolled these coils on top of each other in a round shape.

They would then push onto the clay and use their hands or pieces of wood, stones, and other natural tools to shape and design it into a desired container.

Else they would take handfuls of clay and mold it onto a shape in the palms of their hand. Tribal people would also make handles and feet for some of their pots out of clay. These tribal people used tools such as mussels, shells, or sticks to draw designs, and they used different textures to create a pattern. They rubbed and polished and used techniques, such as wet clay on dry clay products.

Several of these native cultures we are going to discuss made patterns, shapes, and animals in their artwork. The style they often used distinguished their art pieces as a specific tribe or from a certain area. Some tribes were less finicky or artistic, and they preferred a practical plain brown pottery style that was useful.

Mississippian Era

The Mississippian era started around a thousand years ago. This was the start of a more complex art design and shape used in pottery, which had never been seen before. It is thought that there was a group of potters that made orders to sell their wear to an elite group of people.

The ceramic containers were now made up of art pieces that included carinated bowls, salt distilling pans, tripod (three-legged) pots, and more. Let's have a look below at the different tribal designs and methods used.

Cheyenne Earthenware

Most of the Cheyenne tribe lived off the Great Plains, and others stayed in what is now known as Central Minnesota's core regions. The Cheyenne were famous for using bison or buffalo designs in their works of art. The bison products were often used to highlight different elements of their artwork and culture. Yet they also worked with finer products that were superbly crafted, such as the ornamental earthenware pieces that depicted colorful patterns.

Pottery Shoshone

The Shoshone tribe lived throughout America, but mostly in the Eastern parts. This tribe gained horses from the European settlers in the 1700s, and they rose to prominence or fame as a fiercely fighting force of Native Americans.

The Shoshone tribe were skilled potters who loved to use unique methods to produce lovely, useful jugs, bowls, and gourds that they used in their daily life. Shoshone pottery is easily recognizable for its distinctive form and design. This tribe was very artistic and used a lot of color and drawings on their items. They also showed a strong tribal culture, and it was reflected in the patterns they used on the ceramics they made.

Cherokee Ceramic Work

Native American tribes of the Southeastern states, such as the Cherokee, valued their pottery style and art greatly. They created a lot of beautiful art, such as pots, bowls, gourds, plates, as well as jugs.

Instead of using the spinning wheels that we use today, the Cherokee tribe scooped clay from the ground and spent hours shaping and designing it by hand. They used paddles or pieces of flat wood or cloths with water to create a smooth effect.

The distinguishing features of Cherokee pottery are the perfectly smooth surface and the clean, clear designs. They burned the smooth-surfaced pottery on flat stones that were buried in an outdoor fireplace.

Ancient Pueblo Pottery

The Pueblo tribe has produced clay pots for nearly 2,000 years. The craft of pottery-making was passed down the generation, to women, from their more experienced female relatives.

Pueblo pottery can be divided into two basic eras: prehistoric and historic.

The historical period started in the early 16th century when the Spanish settlers arrived. There were three main uses for pottery below:

- Practical cooking, carrying water, storing food, and serving
- Ceremonial occasions
- Commercial sales

Ancient Pueblo pottery was a Black-on-White ceramic type style. The white came from clay hues that were found. The black paint was extracted from iron-rich sediment in rock, and this sediment was called hematite, or plants that were boiled, and this colored water was mixed with clay.

This carried on into the historical period and into the early 20th century. However, the pottery created for trade underwent a new evolution. Many ceramics from the 18th through the 21st century continue to have geometric patterns on them. Some designs had floral patterns or motifs (pictures) depicting animals and birds or representations of other parts of nature, such as the sky, rain, and lightning.

Artwork inspired by animals and the natural world was also linked to myths with religious or historical importance. Pitchers and figurines, for example, were occasionally created in the form of animals or human-like figures. Traditional Pueblo ceramic colors were often orange, white, black, red, and brown.

Navajo Indian Horsehair Ceramics

Traditionally, Navajo containers were heavy and extremely simple, and they were used only for short-term water storage and for drumming. Around 150 years before the arrival of the Spaniards, these hunters and gatherers made their homes in the Southwest.

Vases were made tall and pretty much straight, with only a little cure to them. Yet their art evolved, and they are famous for their horsehair pottery, which was adapted from Acoma Pueblo.

Horsehair is a unique technique that is used where the surface is decorated with horsehair. Hair is placed on pottery that has been heated up from the fire, and this leaves carbon imprints of the hair on the pieces. This also created clear patterned lines when the hairs were burnt onto the surface.

Iroquois Stoneware

The five Native American groups that made up the Iroquois tribe are the Cayuga, Oneida,

Mohawk, Seneca, and Onondaga. They were all located in the Northeastern region of the United States. The Iroquois tribe also produced ceramics with a distinctive style that became a useful design element.

Before the Europeans came, the tribe's ornamental artifacts were created out of natural materials. And these included maize husk, skin, clay, wood, stone, shell, and bone. During European colonization, they changed it to glass, fabric, and metal.

The Iroquois tribe, such as the Cherokee, dug the clay from the earth and sculpted it by hand, although the properties are a little different from the other tribes. Iroquois pottery had a rounder base, and it was black, which shows us that they used a lower temperature when baking their clay.

Modern Native American Pottery

Today Pueblo pottery dominates American Indian ceramics art, although Navajo pottery has recently made a significant comeback. The primary producers of modern Native American pottery include new methods such as Acoma, Santa Clara, Hopi, Jemez, San Ildefonso, and Zia ceramic vessels that you can look up and learn about.

Beadwork

This American Indian art form has a long history, going back to the earliest tribes that beaded patterns long before the arrival of the Europeans. Since its early stages, beading has undergone several major changes. However, it has retained its fame and appeal in North America and elsewhere.

To better understand the history of genuine Native American beading, let's have a good look at it below.

Native American Culture

Native Indians first used beadwork as a form of artistic expression that suited their nomadic way of life. Native American culture shows great importance to ornamental beadwork.

Practical objects that were capable of being packed up and moved easily, such as leather goods belts, jewelry bands, clothing, and horse trappings, were woven with bead patterns and designs. Various Native tribes created their own distinctive beading styles as an expression and trademark.

The Native Americans in North America used a lot of glass beads to decorate. The Navajo tribe, for example, have used glass beads on every piece they have created, from modern works of art and clothing to more traditional gear or clothing worn at powwows ceremonies. This tribe is also known for its weaving and textile abilities.

Making Beads Out of Natural Materials

Early beading started off by cutting natural materials into the shape of beads. Native American bead artisans were once restricted in choice and only used materials that they could find around the area they stayed in.

For instance, natural stones—both precious and non-precious were dug out of the ground. They also used beads that were formed from bones, carved wood, claws, and teeth, sewn onto clothes, or strung together to form necklaces.

Quills were frequently used as beads since they already had a hole through which to string the thread through, and they needed less preparation. In actuality, quillwork itself was regarded as a sacred skill.

Tribes that lived close to the coast would use pearls and shells when beading. The Native Americans used stone tools or rough sand when making beads. It actually required a lot of manual labor from the artisans who shaped the beads and drilled the holes by hand.

The pre-Columbian period saw greater advancements in indigenous beadwork. The tribal people used more hand-ground shells and coral to create their beadwork. One of the main color components of Native American jewelry or beadwork came from the Southwest, and that was the color turquoise. The Northern Shoshone employed vivid colors and the lazy/lane stitch to attach the beadwork. Today a lot of glass, copper, and brass buttons are used in creating their beadwork.

European Settlers Introduced a Style

Native American beading underwent a revolution once the European settlers arrived, and this was thanks to the trade of beads. This was when the little glass beads were introduced into tribal designs.

Indigenous peoples worked quickly as they were talented in beading. They used a variety of hues (colors), patterns, and symbols in their work. The artists challenged themselves by introducing more complex and imaginative designs for commercial trade sales. For these reasons, beadwork has become famous and highly valued - in its vibrant colors and intricate (a lot of detail) designs.

Historically, members of the Crow tribe worked with beads to add to their clothing. They made arm and leg covers, as well as other decorative objects and jewelry. The designers ensured that their artwork would be noticed from a distance, so they used light blue backgrounds in addition to depicting the sky.

The Crow tribe rarely used red beads in their designs due to the additional cost of the beads as well as the unfavorable cultural overtones. Tribal groups had a habit of personalizing everything, from exquisite necklaces that told a story; to the bead choices in belts that were made of buffalo hide.

Native Americans had to combine style and usefulness because they were nomadic, unlike European artists who created art pieces meant to be shown and to decorate rooms in their houses.

Their bead-based artwork was visible in

their everyday clothing, and basic goods, tents, and horse equipment. Early beadwork followed the same basic principles as early quillwork did. Women occasionally received new techniques or designs in dreams from spirits that visited. When they received a new design, it became their personal property, and it could be donated or sold as the dreamer saw fit.

Strangely, the 'reserve period' moved beading to a higher level; this was when Indian beading reached its artistic height of fame that it's known for today. The tribes of the Plains were no longer free to live a nomadic lifestyle as they did before.

They didn't move around anymore, and several tribes were faced with white civilization and close interaction with other Indian tribe members, whom they previously didn't have much contact with and trade with.

This change mostly affected tribes such as the Lakota, Arapahoe, and Cheyenne tribes. This period enhanced a level of creativity in beading that was never seen before. Dresses, pipe bags, cradles, and other accessories were also covered in a brilliance of color. Some designs were regarded as 'tribal property,' as tribal fashions gradually became more distinctive in their appearance.

Many Great Plains Indian women still favored the robustness and comfort of their traditional components, even when steel needles and commercially tanned skins were available. They still feel connected to the past when using bone awls, which are bones that are split into sharp splinters and used as needles, natively tanned hides, and sinew thread.

However, cotton thread is occasionally used as a convenience. Today the central blue pattern serves as a representation of the Great Plains tribal unity. Certain markings, along with the outer band, are known as the 'sky bands,' and the pieces suggest that they are made for a particular purpose, such as a ceremony.

All the outfits are often made from animal skin, such as buffalo hide. The mixture of beadwork and design around the garment's neck served as an expression of the artist's preferences and a mark of ownership.

A current generation of beaders has radically updated their craft, one that has been handed down over the years. Their creations demonstrate that artists can move from their individual community style and produce trendy or modern works by still upholding beading traditions.

Weaving

The Native Indian custom believes that myths and legends brought their weaving abilities and skills. For instance, in some Southwestern communities, they believed the spider's ability to spin webs was passed on to humans when a 'Spider Woman' taught the people how to weave fabric and spin thread.

The Hopis, however, tell a tale about a 'Spider Grandmother' who mindfully created the universe by weaving her web. Below is a technique called finger weaving, which we will investigate.

Finger Weaving

Finger weaving is regarded as one of the genuine folk arts of Native Americans. They wove small strips of fabric — belts, bag straps, sashes, and other objects. This craft is very practical because it doesn't need any specialized equipment like looms.

For finger weaving, one only needs simple wooden sticks and yarn. Auxiliary tools like dowel rods, rubber bands, binder clips, and other items are used today by modern weavers, but they weren't necessary for the time of their ancestors.

Weaving was constructed from a range of local plant materials using only an awl (small sharp tool) and a knife. Tribes also used weather coiling, which is a technique that combines the wrapping of base material with a sewing style.

The Southwestern tribes are known for their distinctively patterned coiled baskets. These skillful craftspeople have moved traditional basket coiling to another level of excellence.

Threads are twined or rounded together and sown in a method to create a weave pattern called twining. In all basket-making villages, weavers and their families tend to a variety of harvests and plant ceremonies every year, where their weaving plays a big role. Plants that were used to weave with were willow, conifer, sedge, roots, grasses, ferns, yucca, and redbud.

It often took as long to prepare the weaving materials as it did to actually weave the fabric.

The Native Americans' way of existence permanently changed with historical events since the first contact with Europeans.

The massive influx of new people and their diverse land-use practices have made traditional basketry a thing of the past. Due to their changing environment, many weavers stopped weaving products for personal reasons, and some started manufacturing baskets for sale.

Process Of Weaving

Early European Americans appreciated North American art and became interested in their Indigenous basketry. During the same time, popular architectural and interior design styles were created. The native designs were bought in as treasured decorative art. Unknowingly, foreign customers actually contributed to the development of Indian basketry in those days.

The weaving changed shape and style to fill a preference for a select collector. Realistic motives or images of pictures of butterflies, flowers, animals, and humans began being woven into basketry. Often, these new designs were also mixed with older designs. By weaving a variety of patterns, the weavers displayed a higher level of skill.

Over time, woven products became strong and light, which made them ideal for the annual subsistent (small farming) lifestyles that many Indian tribes historically lived in at the time. Food resources were gathered, prepared, and cooked using a variety of basketry techniques.

Beautiful baskets were decorated with colorful feathers, beads, shells, pearls, and wool. Magnificently woven pieces were presented for significant occasions like weddings, rituals, and other rites of passage. The weaving showed incredible creative talent and meticulous attention to detail in all its forms, which was thought to reach far beyond their true functional ability.

Today the finest basketry in the world is made by American Indians. Artistic expression flourishes in the diverse styles of their daily life. The Yokut tribe, for instance, often creates a dynamic pattern on their cooking baskets, while the superbly crafted Aleut baskets show sophistication like no other.

In fact, the spectacular Haida motifs are so eye-catching you battle to keep from staring at them. Baskets are still used in ceremonial events, as well as for a few practical reasons. Why not consider asking your parents to add clay or a beading kit as an option to the gift ideas this year? So you can explore your creative side!

CHAPTER 6
NATIVE AMERICAN GAMES AND SPORTS

Games and sports were created to bring unity and fun to the native communities. What sports do you play? Sports and games are important, as they provide good exercise, teach you about yourself and other people around you, and are fun to play.

Games and sports help you become skilled in movement, building you as a person. They also benefit other areas of your life that you would never consider. These active events helped the tribe's men to stay fit and prepared for any action. Later other reasons were included in these activities. Below are a few main sports events that were created by the Native Indians.

Lacrosse

Lacrosse is a fun game and originally started as stickball, a Native Indian invention. This game was originally played by tribal warriors for training, entertainment, as well as religious reasons. This game has been expanded into a profession and a global sport.

The Algonquian tribe invented the game and first practiced it in the St. Lawrence Valley region. Other tribes from the Eastern half of North America and other regions around the Western Great Lake areas began to play lacrosse.

The Native American games were eventually seen as a major occasion, which took place over several days. Many tribes would come together and compete with one another. A goal area was established, by heaping rocks on top of each other or using two trees, alongside one another. The Native Indians played over vast open spaces between villages, anywhere from 500 yards to several miles apart.

There were many players, anywhere from 100 to 100,000 contestants, all playing at the same time. They made set boundaries, and after that, only two straightforward rules were created:

- The first rule was a person hurled a ball into the air to signify the beginning of the match, and players raced to be among the

first to get to it.
- The second rule was your hands were not allowed to connect with the ball.

The traditional wooden balls were later exchanged for a deerskin ball that was packed with fur. The sticks were developed into more of a complex tool, and netting was made from deer sinew. Players used paint and charcoal on their bodies and faces before the games started.

In 1636, Jean de Brébeuf described a sport being played by Huron Indians in a book he wrote, and he gave the game a name and called it, 'lacrosse.' Then the Caughnawaga Indians were invited to travel to Montreal in 1834 and play lacrosse, which they did.

As a result, this sport started to become popular in Canada. The Montreal Lacrosse Club was established in 1856 by a Canadian dentist, Dr. William George Beers (Wikipedia, 2020). After a decade, Beers drafted rules that included a limited group of players, and he added a rubber ball and redesigned the stick.

In 1867 exhibition matches took place in England, and by 1860 lacrosse had become Canada's national sport. A touring Canadian team and the 'Iroquois-made team' both traveled to Scotland in 1883.

Lacrosse was played in the Summer Olympics in 1904 and 1908, gaining a lot more popularity at the beginning of the 20th century. Lacrosse games have been accepted by other nations and adapted into different sports that are still played today (Claydon, n.d.).

Shinny

The tribal people responsible for creating this awesome sport were the Saux, Foxes, and Assiniboine tribes. Do you know the game called ice hockey? I'm quite sure you do, but did you know that this sport you love to play or watch was derived from shinny? The game 'shinny' is actually a casual variation of ice hockey.

The Native Americans used a curved stick to smack a deerskin ball down the field. It was thought that this sport took place on the ice in the winter months and land in the summer, but many now believe the game was only played on land.

White settlers saw the Native Americans play, and they were fascinated by the sport and kept track of it.

Eventually, shinny evolved into what is now known as ice hockey. There are a few differences to the hockey game of today, but it's virtually the same idea (Wikipedia Contributors, 2019b).

There were no nets, and the tribal people used organic things, such as stones or trees, to mark the goal area on each end. Certain gameplay was not allowed since there was a lack of safety clothing on the players:

- Body checking: a defensive play in which a player attempts to get the puck away from a rival teammate. A check is when a defensive player intentionally moves in the opposing or the same direction as the puck is being carried and strikes the player hard with his upper body.
- Reefing/raising the puck/roofing and shooting the puck or ball above the ice is not prohibited.

Shinny was informal in its early stages - pucks and sticks were frequently handmade or picked up. For instance, during the Great Depression, Northern youngsters used tin cans, pieces of wood, and sometimes even frozen horse droppings as pucks. Any item could be used as a puck if it was the appropriate size.

The term actually comes from the Scottish game 'shinty.' In the United States, 'shinny,' is typically referred to as 'pick-up hockey' or 'pond hockey.'

All levels of hockey fans can enjoy playing

this game, which requires a small ice rink, a few pieces of equipment, and only the skill to grasp a stick and, if possible, at the very least, an attempt to contact the passing ball or puck.

Shinny was created as a purely enjoyable and non-competitive sport. For instance, there is often no goaltender. Today, certain local governments around the world use paid-out taxes to formally construct and maintain ice rinks, just for ice hockey or shinny.

Many rinks are built and maintained by public employees all through the winter, namely in Montreal, Edmonton, Quebec, Alberta, Canada, Calgary, and Edmonton. The city of Toronto also offers programs for adults, so they can gain experience when playing shinny or casual hockey in a rink. Amazingly, lessons are often free or inexpensive. Toronto offers fifty-four outdoor artificially cooled rinks, far more than any other city in the world (Orlega, 2020).

You don't need to wear the entire kit, either. Below you will see what rules have been established:

- All athletes have to wear hockey helmets.
- If you are younger than 19, you must wear a full-face guard.
- All competitors are strongly advised to

wear hockey gloves and a neck protector.
- You need to bring your own sticks, skates, and pucks to the game.
- There are no goalies in the match.

Stickball

Native American stickball is known as a team sport that is usually played on an open field. It is similar to the sport of lacrosse. A tribal dance was often held the evening before the game, and the majority of the town participated.

The dances included spiritual songs and rituals, as well as 'conjuring-up' ceremonies, that were thought to bring the team luck. To scare rivals, the players shouted religious sentiments and made sacrifices while wearing ceremonial garb.

The medicine man would perform ceremonies to prepare the players and their equipment (sticks and pucks). The shaman would withdraw each participant from the dance, one at a time, to carry out the 'mystic rite known as, going to the water,' at which point he would bless the activity and give each participant ritualistic scratches that were also thought to 'create' luck.

The shaman would encourage the team to win by allowing 'the blood to flow freely' throughout the contest. The game was often played to settle a conflict with another clan or tribal community member.

The Choctaw tribe played stickball, using a ball that was made with woven leather, and it was called a towa, and handcrafted sticks called kabocca. Without ever touching or tossing the ball into the air, each team attempted to move the ball down the field toward the goalpost of the opposing team.

When his ball was hit by the opponent's team, the player hit the ball. This sport was carried out by many tribes of the American indigenous people, including the Coconki tribe, Yuchi, Chickasaw, Seminole, Choctaw and Muscogee. The number of participants in the game is not large. However, there should be equal number of athletes on the field, usually thirty on each side.

This sport is carried out in one field, and there are usually three groups of players in the game. The first group will hold each other from the goal, and they are called "roses" because they protect their goals.

The second group is positioned in the middle of the field, and this player is in charge of pushing the ball down the field toward the goal.

The third group is known as the "returners," and they congregate around the opposing team's pole in order to assist their team in scoring points on the opposite team's pole.

Injuries often occurred, as there were a large number of players, and they were all trying to get to one ball. Stickball is and has always been a full-contact sport, played without safety equipment, such as helmets or padding, and in many instances, without shoes.

The earlier games also had a fairly limited set of rules. This game was actually used as a peaceful conflict method, yet deaths did occur. Today stickball injuries are rare and widespread, but there are more regulations to stop players from suffering life-threatening injuries.

The most popular guidelines are: no one touches the ball, no swinging of sticks is allowed at anyone, and no striking below the knees. Another rule is the player tackling the player in control of the ball should drop his stick first.

Today's game is played on a field that is approximately 100 yards long, and there are tall cylindrical poles that serve as goals - on either side of the field. By racing through the set of poles with the ball or while holding the game sticks and in control of the ball, players can score points. In casual games, scoring is not often scored strictly.

The popularity of stickball has grown to such an extent that various tribe competitions, including Choctaw Labor Day Celebration and the Jim Thorpe Games, which are conducted annually across the country.

The World Series is 'undoubtedly the largest and most fiercely contested Indigenous ballgame in the country,' and it is hosted by the Mississippi band of Choctaws in Mississippi and in Philadelphia.

We should all be grateful to the Native Americans for sharing their exciting games with us, as it has brought a lot of income and enjoyment into our lives.

CHAPTER 7
FAMOUS NATIVE AMERICAN LANDMARKS AND PLACES

In this chapter, we will discover the heritage sites of the Native Americans. I believe it's the responsibility of everyone living in America to treat the locations we visit with respect. We don't need to believe in the indigenous faith of the Native Americans for us to try and protect these special areas.

The high value that is contained in these places cannot be explained. Sacred or holy locations take beliefs beyond the private sphere of one's conscience; they are special places where beliefs are made to last. Below are a few cultural or heritage sites.

Mesa Verde National Park

Mesa Verde National Park is known as a sacred area. The Mesa Verde's cliffs and mesas mean it's an individual ridge, hill, or slope with a flat top that is surrounded on all sides. The steep rocky cliffs rise noticeably above its surroundings.

The mesas have been home to the vibrant Ancient Pueblo civilizations for more than 700 years. The National Park now preserves and cares for the rich cultural legacy of twenty-six tribal groups and provides tourists with an eye-opening and breathtaking view into the past.

There are nearly a thousand species of plants living in this World Heritage Site. Some of these species are found nowhere else and are unique to the area. In 550 CE, Pueblo inhabitants made their way to the region of Mesa Verde National

Park. They were nomadic people with a changing way of life. These skilled basket weavers went on to take up another skill in pottery. Today, these two artistic skills mentioned rank among the best in the world.

They also learned how to grow crops such as corn, beans and squash, and they added to their diet when collecting fruit and wild plants. They also sourced their required protein from the animals they hunted. They hunted mostly deer, rabbits, birds, and squirrels in the Mesa Verde region.

Their homes started off in pit houses, which were alcoves dug into the ground in the mesas. Later, as the tribe grew in population, they built larger adobe homes, known as pueblos.

Adobe is buildings created from organic resources, such as straw, dirt, or clay. Adobe is the Spanish word for 'mudbrick,' and adobe-built structures look similar to enormous bricks. Yet there were smaller single houses that were also built.

By the year 1000, people were building multi-story stone buildings everywhere. The population of Mesa Verde increased to several thousand individuals between 1100 and 1300, with the majority living in close-knit communities with several rooms.

The 'Four Corners region' shows the imprints of the ancestral Pueblo people, who left behind these massive dwellings, villages, and cultural artifacts. Some people started returning to the cliffside alcoves in the late 1100s.

So, it's estimated that these cliff homes were built between the late 1190s and the late 1270s, and they ranged in size from one-room constructions to huge communities that looked similar to Cliff Palaces and Longhouse. A large house could have around a hundred and fifty rooms in it.

These buildings were fitted into or built into any available space. Living rooms typically measured six by eight feet, and they provided space for two to three people. It's likely they also had smaller storage spaces at the back, on the upper floor. The majority of settlements had underground kivas, which are believed to have served a ceremonial purpose.

Huge changes began to happen in the Pueblo tribe's world in the 1200s. On and around Mesa Verde, many residents migrated or moved to larger, safer communities. Some started to relocate away from the area altogether, while others settled away of the Mesa tops into the cliff homes.

Archaeological evidence suggests that these changes may have been influenced by a string of events such as droughts, a loss of resources, and social unrest. So, it's possible that the population moved away as a result of conflict, agricultural failures, or the loss of heavily exploited soils, greenwoods, and diminished wildlife.

By the 1280s, the sounds of life and building had spread Southward toward the present-day Pueblos, which is located on the Hopi mesas in Arizona, along the River Grande, and its tributaries in New Mexico. The once-bustling Mesa Verde area basically became unpopulated by the end of the 13th century. The tribal people moved among settled relatives who were already staying in New Mexico and Arizona.

Why not tell your parents that you want to spend a night at the Morefield and go camping or stay over at the Far View Lodge? The Montezuma Valley, Park Point, and geologic overhead views provide Mesa Verde Park with a wonderful setting and scenery as you enter.

The Chapin Mesa, or Wetherill Mesa, is also filled with ancestral sites that can be accessed by the general public. Try and encourage your family to schedule time at Wetherill Mesa and Chapin Mesa during the summer months. In the winter season, Wetherill Mesa is closed to the public.

There are so many areas to stay in, with beautiful views and things to do. For instance, the Spruce Tree House, Cliff Palace, Balcony House, and Far View locations. They also supply self-guided driving tours along Mesa's top loop road, all of which are in the area of Chapin Mesa, which offer views of the cliffside homes.

This National Historic Landmark makes for a wonderful vacation with all its fantastic things to do and finds and ample amounts of amenities such as restrooms and food service that cater to your every need.

Chaco Canyon

Chaco Culture National Historical Park is

the homeland of the Navajo Indians of the Southwest, the Hopi Indians of Arizona, and the Pueblo Indians of New Mexico. It had been discovered that between AD 850 and 1250, the Chaco Canyon was a significant Puebloan cultural hub.

The park is placed in a canyon that is carved out by a natural Chaco wash, and it's located towards the Northwest part of New Mexico and halfway between Albuquerque and Farmington.

This archaeological site is guarded by an overhanging cliff face that indicates the first dated proof of human life in Chaco Canyon. The materials and finds that have become dateable are also protected in this area. The canyon looks as though there were people living in it for many hundreds of years. So, there's a big possibility that prehistoric tribal people hunted and gathered all around this area.

The ceremonial buildings are colossal in size, and they have unusual multi-story buildings called 'great homes,' that have also served in the center's ceremonies, political discussions, and trade.

It has been estimated that between 1150 and 1250, people stopped building 'great houses' and started to move to new areas. These inhibitors moved into areas such as the Hopi of Arizona and became part of the Pueblo Peoples of New Mexico, and several others still had ties to the Chaco tribes today.

The brilliantly planned out area, and well-built houses, which included multi-story designs, are of high-end craftsmanship. This shows us the extent of the Chaco social structures and the advancement of their skill. These structures stand out within the local cultures of the ancient Pueblo people and a few other small tribes.

It is thought that these tribes ruled the region for more than four centuries. The ancient Puebloan people built enormous structures and highway systems, leaving proof of how gifted they were in engineering. Their planning skills and creativity have also been unheard of in this period. Several of these well-designed and crafted network highways that were carefully built and connected to sites can be clearly seen today. The very difficult and cruel environment makes the achievements even more impressive and noteworthy.

All the archaeological parts that have been found were needed to explain and help us understand the brilliant universal store load that makes up the Chaco Culture. Structures were five or more stories high, and their walls were made of sandstone and mud mortar (mud, water, lime, volcanic ash, or Portland cement). They had pine roof beams and extremely well-preserved archaeological finds, which helped us in reliving a great part of this culture. Chaco Culture is unique in terms of its shapes and patterns, as well as the materials and content found, and then to be framed in a mind-blowing setting is awesome.

The area has been excellently preserved, and many of its walls, equipment, personal effects, furnishings, materials, and other objects still exist in their original settings. Most of these components have survived the weather conditions and the centuries, and this has been pinned down to the brilliant workmanship and the dry location that this tribe built in.

The history and finds indicate the Navajo tribe stayed in the wider area in the 1600s. However, there is also proof of a lot of settlement patterns that were found, at the same time, in the canyon.

Some of these findings show us that the Navajo or Dine people may have arrived at Chaco Canyon a lot earlier than was thought. In 1680, the Pueblo Rebellion briefly brought the neighboring Pueblo tribes together in New

Mexico. Nonetheless, the region was once again conquered and overtaken by the Spaniards in 1692. Many of the Pueblo people were driven into exile as a result.

So many of these individuals looked for safety among the Navajo in Chaco Canyon and its neighborhood. They exchanged ideas, and they inter-married into different tribes. Archaeologists have found weaponry that explains that the Navajo ruins in the canyon lived through a time of conflict or war.

In 1774, Don Bernardo de Mieray Pacheco labeled the Chaco Canyon region on a Spanish map as 'Chaca' (Wikipedia, 2023). Jose Antonio Viscarra, the Spanish governor of New Mexico, led a military force to the West of Jemez Pueblo, in Navajo territory. As he journeyed, he saw many Chacoan structures.

For several weeks, Bureau Victor and Cosmos Mindeleff, who were part of the American Ethnology employees, inspected the area and documented and took many pictures of the main Chacoan sites; these images have helped with early records.

In 1896-1900, Richard Wetherill asked for permission to dig out areas (Wikipedia, 2023). His argument was that areas and sites on cliff dwellings in Mesa Verde and other ancient Puebloan sites had already been dug out. The formation of the Hyde Exploration Expedition was given the go-ahead. They undertook a sizable dig-out at Pueblo Bonito under the direction of Richard Wetherill, who had received funding.

Today, the park shows - how visitors, industry, and the environment's elements have all affected the sites negatively, with all its vandalism and looting. In 2012, the completion of the park's new visitor center took place, yet the park remains a site of research.

In 2009, chocolate remnants or crumbs were found in Pueblo Bonito cylinder jars. (State Museum Arizona, n.d.) The researchers have also discovered the first traces of chocolate to come from the North of the US-Mexico border, and this connected Mesoamerica to Chacoan rituals that involved the use of cacao.

Patricia Crown of the University of New Mexico said that these are part of the priceless artifacts that have been found in mounds that surrounded Pueblo Bonito, which were originally dug out in the 1920s. The park continues to safeguard these very important areas by keeping a close eye on the locations with the assistance of volunteer groups and students.

You can go on guided tours now and on hiking trails into the hills or take a fun bike ride. Be part of fun-filled evening campfire talks and activities and watch the beautiful night sky. All of these activities will create a closer connection with the canyon and its past, where thousands of people once lived.

The property is big enough and ensures you will see all the elements, and the past is well showcased. The ancient Puebloan culture is a must-see, with its picturesque setting in the Chaco Canyon.

You will see why it's famous for its colossal buildings, brilliant artistic designs and unusual architecture, astronomy, and all the tribe's accomplishments. It's definitely unlike anything that has come before; what a gift it is to visit the Four Corners District.

Grand Canyon National Park

In Northern Arizona, the memorable Grand Canyon National Park covers 278 miles (447 km) of the Colorado River and is surrounded by hilly areas.

Did you know that the state of Rhode Island is only about 1,212 square miles, while the park measures a whopping 1,904 square miles? The canyon itself measures more than a mile deep and ten miles broad in certain areas. It takes around four hours just to journey 200 miles (320 km) from the North Rim Visitor Center to the South Rim Visitor Center.

Although geologists disagree on some points regarding the size of the canyon's parts, that are missing and how many years it took to develop. A number of recent studies prove that the idea of the Colorado River's first formation and the course it made through the region was between 5 and 6 million years ago (Wikipedia Contributors, 2019g).

Since then, the Colorado River has caused the tributaries to be cut and the cliffs to retreat, and at the same time, this has caused a deepening into the canyon, enlarging it. The Grand Canyon is a river valley in the Colorado Plateau and one of the six main sections of the Colorado Plateau province. Although the Grand Canyon is not the deepest canyon in the world (the deeper canyon is the Kali Gandaki Gorge in Nepal), it is renowned for its enormous size and beauty.

The canyon's temperature varies dramatically; it can shift by more than 25 degrees from the outer rim to the lowest point in the West of the canyon. Whereas the depth of the gorge reaches great heat in the summer. The North Rim will then often drop below freezing in the winter months.

Spanish explorer Garcia López de Cárdenas, who arrived in the area in 1540, is thought to have been the first European to see the Grand Canyon (National Clothing, 2018). Its thick succession of old rocks, which has been well preserved, is exposed in the canyon walls, making this a memorable geological perspective.

These rock layers preserve a large part of the early geological history of North America. These sediments raised from mountain buildings that constitute the Colorado Plateau.

The buoyancy of the Kaibab Plateau cut in Grand Canyon in COLORADO PLATEAU in North Rand is almost 300 m from North Rand, North Rand. (300 m).

Although most of the drainage flows on the plateau flow out of the canyon behind the south, almost the entire drainage is from North Rand (also receiving more rain and snow) to the Grand Canyon (according to the general tendency). As a result, the tributary and canyons on the north side are longer, deeper, while the south side is cleaner and the side is steeper.

This area has been ancestral land for eleven affiliated tribes. The Puebloan people were the first known inhabitants of the area and stayed around the Grand Canyon. Although the present Puebloan peoples dislike the title 'Anasazi,' the cultural group has frequently been called the Anasazi in archaeology. Anasazi is Navajo for 'enemy ancestors' or 'foreign ancestors,' depending on the context.

When this particular culture first emerged is

still up for discussion. Native Indians have been inhabiting the region continuously for thousands of years and have established settlements inside the canyon and in its many caves. The Grand Canyon was held with honor by the Pueblo people, who undertook pilgrimages there. The Grand Canyon is also regarded as a portal to the afterlife by the Hopi People.

The location has long held deep spiritual importance for the people. They believe after passing away (death), a person travels to the afterlife by passing through the special place of 'emergence' located upstream in the canyon. This is where Colorado and Little Colorado Rivers meet.

The rock squirrel has been the most hazardous creature in the canyon! Visitors are most frequently bitten by this common squirrel, despite the fact that there are also Gila monsters and bighorn sheep living there.

The Grand Canyon is the most spectacular and amazing example of erosion in the entire world. The views it gives visitors from the rim are breathtakingly beautiful. It's another must-see! The South Rim is accessible all year, but the North Rim is closed in winter. Go and see the Grand Canyon; it's the most well-known canyon in the world.

CHAPTER 8
NATIVE AMERICAN TRIBES TODAY

There are many different groups that fall under American Indians that are still in America today. Each tribe has its own worldview, language, culture, and method when producing art, food, and medicine. These tribes still shared traits and issues that have formed the basis for their conflict and international policies.

Native tribes have gone through a lot of hardship: as they have lost a lot of family members; their homes, their culture; and their way of life. American Indian populations were swiftly driven from their ancestral lands as a result of a flood of American colonizers that moved in and wanted to create an industry. These tribes were forced from the North to the Southern parts of the United States.

This displacement came through treaties and political scheming. Other times it came about by force. In 1816, the Choctaw leaders were persuaded to exchange some of their ancestral territories, which were positioned towards the East of the Tombigbee River. Then again, in 1820, they were told to surrender a considerable amount of their holdings.

In May 1829, the Indian Removal Act was brought to Congress by a representative from the South (Drexler, 2019). It included Native tribes from the Southeast of the United States, such as the Choctaw, Chickasaw, Cherokee, Creek, and Seminole tribes.

At this time, Washington, D.C., received hundreds of petitions arguing that this action was wrong, damaging, and immoral. Yet, President Andrew Jackson and the U.S. Congress eventually passed the Act with only five votes.

All of these tribes mentioned above went through a terrible trail as they walked a tortuous distance through horrible areas in dreadful weather conditions. The Choctaw tribe suffered immensely since they were the first American Indian tribe to be relocated. The Choctaw tribe walked from Oklahoma to Mississippi, and it was a tough journey that claimed many lives along the way.

As many as 3,000 people died on these horrific trips from a group of about 70,000 people. This journey was eventually named the 'Trail of Tears.' Today, this despicable event is spoken about in honor. The honor is directed toward the bravery shown by these forced tribe members who endured such hardship.

Tribes That Still Exist Today

There are five hundred and seventy-four individual genuine tribes living in the United States today. These tribes surround forty-eight states, as well as parts of Alaska. The Bureau of Indian Affairs provides cash and services to these federally recognized tribes directly or indirectly through contracts, grants, and other agreements.

These monetary offers are mostly for the upkeep and preservation of the heritage site and for further investigation into the Native American culture. Large groups of Indigenous Mexican Americans have now set up residence along the U.S.-Mexico border. The tribes include the Cocopah, Pai, and Yaqui, and they often move across the boundary that divides their traditional homelands.

With five hundred and seventy-four tribes, it

will be difficult to mention them all, but we can discuss the largest groups living in America today (Smithers, 2015).

The Cherokee Tribe

The Cherokee tribe is by far the largest tribe that stays in America today. This tribe once lived in the modern-day Southern states, and they are called North and South Carolina, South and West Virginia, Kentucky, Georgia, Tennessee, and Alabama.

Cherokee tribal people don't live on reservation land any longer. The word reserve means a piece of land given to a Native tribe by the government in exchange for the land they lived on before.

Instead, the tribal members bought 57,000 acres of land in the 1800s. In this Indian territory, the Cherokee established a new administration and educational system. However, when Oklahoma became a state in 1907, the U.S. government destroyed these established institutions.

Besides these losses, the Cherokee eventually grew to be the largest tribe in America and maintained a high standard of living. Today, the Eastern Band of Cherokee Indians possess territory that is known as the

Qualla Boundaries, and the federal government holds it in trust for them. However, the American Indians feel it's belittling to keep land in a trust, and they are fighting to retain full ownership.

The Qualla boundary includes pristine mountains, forests, and long-flowing rivers as the 'Great Smoky Mountains' border their boundary. As of the beginning of the twenty-first century, the Cherokee Nation's tribal holdings in Northeastern Oklahoma cover 124,000 acres throughout fourteen counties.

This area is held in trust by the American government and is regarded as a Jurisdictional Service Area, despite the fact that it's not a reserve. The majority of Cherokee tribes were staying in North Carolina, Tennessee, and Northeastern Oklahoma by the year 2000.

Many Americans today have a hazy notion of their Native American origin, and Phelps is one of them. However, his recollection was oddly clear on one issue: his Indian identity came from his 'Cherokee blood' line (Smithers, 2015). The practice of declaring a Cherokee ancestor is still practiced today. More Americans now claim to have at least one Cherokee ancestor, more than any other Native American group.

Americans recall and exchange tales of long-lost Cherokee ancestors all around the country. These family stories become less clear with each passing generation, but tribal members such as Phelps, who is a modern American Indian, profess' his belief, even when battling to link a Cherokee member to his clan of ancestor ship. Tribes have all merged or come together at one stage in history.

The Eastern Cherokee still practice their musical skills, storytelling, dancing, culinary skills, basket-making, pottery, beadwork, flint-knapping or tool-making, blowgun-making, and other cultural traditions today.

Members of tribes can cast ballots in local, state, and federal elections without help from the federal government. The Cherokee tribe financially supports their own schools, water supply, sewage system, fire brigade, and emergency responders.

Their language is being reintroduced into classrooms and in society after being outlawed by federal schools for more than 50 years. The Cherokee language is taught in Cherokee schools today. In actuality, the New Kituwah Language Academy only instructs lessons in the Cherokee language (Smithers, 2015).

The Navajo Tribe

The Navajo tribe lives in the Four Corners territory of Utah, Colorado, New Mexico, and Arizona, in the Southwest of the current United States. The Navajo Tribe is very large and has the second-largest total of American Indian members in an area of 27,000 square miles of reservation land.

The Navajo people view the Mesa Verde region as a part of their larger world since it's located within the region that is framed by the four sacred mountains. More than two hundred and fifty thousand Navajo members live off-reservation land today (Crow Canyon, 2023).

The majority of Navajos are English speakers, and they work in the larger American economy, yet they still uphold their own culture, traditions, and religion. When traveling through Navajo land, it's not uncommon to encounter traditional hogans or traditional dwellings. Today these ancient dwellings occasionally stand adjacent to modern houses. There are also sheepherders on horseback that tend to their flocks over the open range.

Handmade products, such as jewelry, pottery, and rugs, have become a big industry for these tribes throughout the twenty-first century. Additionally, a large number of

Navajos work for the local government, as well as in companies, schools, energy, and petroleum industries.

Diné College's Shiprock campus, located at the Southernmost tip of the Mesa Verde area, gives Navajo students a chance to learn about their language, history, and culture while also earning a range of degrees and certificates, to further their options in life.

The Latin American Indians

This tribe is said to make up the third largest group, and over half of its members live in urban areas today. The two main groups that fall under the Latin American heading are the Arawaks and Caribs tribes. Compared to tribes that live in the reserves, these tribal people stay in less-than-safe urban areas, which have poor hygiene, and are disaster-prone neighborhoods.

This tribal community is the most vulnerable of all the tribes, and they often struggle with financial problems that keep occurring. Even though many skills have been taught, and significant development has taken place in the last ten years, a lot more needs to be done to improve the quality of their lives.

The other reason for the Latin American tribes being negatively impacted is that they fall into a low-skilled working bracket, and they are often in unstable positions. We need to see these indigenous peoples through new lenses and consider their voices, customs, and identities in order to lessen their dangers and concerns.

Choctaw Tribe

The Choctaw tribes make up the fourth largest group of tribal members to date. Nowadays, there are two main groups that make up the Choctaw tribes. One group lives in a reserve in Mississippi, which is a territory owned and governed by the tribe.

This group believes that the most vital part of keeping a strong, resilient tribal kingdom is to have the opportunity to choose their own course and to build a society that their forefathers envisioned for the Choctaw Tribes.

The Choctaws of Oklahoma, however, stay on trust property. This is similar to a small country; every Choctaw tribe has a separate governing body - which are a set of laws, their own police force, and community services. Yet the Choctaw tribe must still abide by U.S. law because they are also U.S. citizens.

The Choctaws tribe was formerly governed by a council that was made up of two chiefs from each Choctaw band. This is similar to senators and governors; the Choctaw chief and council members are currently chosen by the people.

The Choctaw people were formerly living in the Southeastern United States, especially in Alabama, Louisiana, Florida, and Mississippi. The first group of Choctaw people to arrive in the reserve used fire to support and regrow their wild plant populations.

They also modified or changed certain areas and cleaned up their local environment. Shannon McDaniel, the director of agribusiness for the Choctaw Nation, said, "Choctaws were largely farmers, and they traded what they grew along the Mississippi river" (Biskinik Newspaper, 2022). The tribes bartered for the things they needed and hunted wild game and harvested food from their gardens to survive.

Families have little, private plots positioned between their homes, where they raise mainly squash, beans, tomatoes, and corn. The tribe itself also shares enormous communal fields for bigger crop varieties.

In the earlier years, their diet mainly consisted of grain, which enabled them to survive the winter. According to Shannon McDaniel, they would store their products for the colder months, and they never ran out. As a result, corn and cornmeal are used to make many of their dishes.

He also claims they consumed a lot of their locally grown produce, such as berries and fruit, as well as their sugar cane crops. This tribe also makes the most beautiful basketry and beaded work to sell, and this supplements their way of life.

They are a determined group of tribal members that fight to bring everything to good in their lives as they contribute towards their historical legacy. Additionally, they are persistent in discovering places to develop their careers. As they pride themselves in their strong core values, and with these factors, they achieve amazing benefits.

The Choctaw Nation is very committed to fostering development and prosperity, as these ideas are consistent with their mission of "Living out the Chahta Spirit of faith, family, and culture" (Biskinik Newspaper, 2022).

The majority of these members have a good understanding of English. They also have an emblem seal that represents their tribe, which was formalized in 1857. This emblem typically represents their neighborhood partnerships. It also depicts the Choctaw tribes' love for peace and preparedness to go to war if attacked. As this is symbolic in the unstrung bow and the tobacco smoke rising from the pipe. Yet the smoke not only represents peace but a connection to one's spiritual life.

The Choctaw Chiefs Pushmataha, Apukshunnubbee, and Moshulatubbee are also represented in the emblem, as they are honored with the three arrows depicted.

Colonization Changed Eskimo Hunting

Historically, the Inuit tribes hunted with swift, nimble tiny boats made of sealskin, named a kayak, a name that is still used today. These indigenous people relied only on the land and the water up until around fifty years ago, as there was a high value placed on hunting.

Today's economy is different, and hunting is no longer the main way of life in Greenland. The majority of Inuit have switched to salary employment in order to pay for electricity and other conveniences.

Yet, the hunting lifestyle, techniques, and cuisine continue to play a large role in their culture and way of life. The Eskimo tribes' manner of life changed because of colonization. In the early 1700s, contracts were set up with

European whalers, and by the early 1800s, these tribes saw the beginning of relationships with the explorers.

Inuit lifestyles underwent significant modifications during the 20th century. The European tools were far more effective than the indigenous tools the tribes made, as they were made of steel. Hunters began to rely more on firearms and motorized transportation instead of traditional tools and dogsleds. Hunting became even less profitable as the food was imported from countries other than the Arctic. So, tribal tool-making decreased dramatically, and the reliance on European commodities became apparent. This dependence grew in time as a result of trading in the Hudson's Bay area.

Arctic sovereignty became a growing source of worry for the federal government throughout the Cold War, and they were determined to change it.

As a result, the Distant Early Warning (DEW) system line was built along the Arctic coast, and it extended from Alaska Eastward to Baffin Island and onwards to Greenland. The DEW Line harmed Inuit people as it now contaminated and changed the Arctic terrain.

The tribal children were sent to boarding

schools, and they lost touch with their traditional lifestyle, which included gathering food supplies. The law was another reason why socio-economic developments played a role in the decline of their culture.

Laws that governed hunting became an even larger barrier–when the Eskimos tried to access their traditional food sources. The federal government started to restrict hunting to protect species that are at risk from climate change. Animal rights groups stepped in, and despite their good intentions, their proposals and demands clashed with traditional Eskimo tribes' beliefs. It's sad, but what's left of these tribes' way of life is being threatened by this collision of civilizations.

Certain actions are, however, being taken to create a solution. The World Heritage List has united with UNESCO to safeguard Caribou hunting, as this is vital to the subsistence of the local populations.

The Inuit continue to eat reindeer, seal, and walrus, as is customary in their diet. Some traditionalists also battle to use modern materials when making their clothes and boots.

Most continue to use traditional hunting trophies, such as polar bears and reindeer skins, yet occasionally, they do use modern materials. Several of the male tribe members are still skilled in age-old hunting techniques, such as kayaking and harpoon tossing.

Hunting for the Inuit tribe is an integral part of their mythology, social structure, identity, and even genetic makeup. For instance, they eat a diet that is high in fat and protein, and they need this specific diet. It's been established that they have an effective fat metabolism that is unlike the Europeans. This means their bodies burn fat a lot faster than the Europeans' bodies do (Science Daily, 2015).

Tallying up the total number of Inuit and Yupik members is challenging, as the terrain is so vast and treacherous. However, it's believed there are over two hundred thousand members, and the majority of these groups stay close to their historic circumpolar homeland. Furthermore, it is estimated that as of 2010, there are 53,785 tribes staying in the U.S., 65,025 in Canada, and 51,730 in Greenland (Wikipedia Contributors, 2019).

Yupik Tribes

Yupik tribe families used to spend the spring and summer in a fish camp before joining others at a community site for the winter. At the community site, the tribes would share their catch and have fellowship with one another. However, smaller tribes still travel in family groups, in search of food supplies, throughout spring, summer, and fall.

Several families also continue to gather food to add as their subsistence foods. When hunting, their particular favorites included Pacific salmon and seal varieties. The community's hub for celebrations and ceremonial rites still exists to an extent, and this includes storytelling, singing, and dancing.

A Traditional Way of Life

Today, most Indian Americans don't make homes out of teepees, igloos, or any other traditional buildings. They do, however, occasionally use these homes for religious purposes.

There are times when they simply love to go back in time and do as their ancestors did since it makes them feel more connected to the past and their great-grandparents. Much like some of us who prepare our family's Christmas cake recipe and some of our late grandmother's pies or fudge, this makes us think and feel connected to grandma.

A Modern Lakota Tribe Member at a POW Ceremony

Situations Are Improving Slowly

Many tribal American lives have improved nowadays, thanks to their self-determination and initiative with the government. However, there are still a number of pressing concerns and problems that need to be solved.

When the European settlers arrived, tribal people lived in villages apart from them. Established American Indian tribes were then regarded as semi-independent nations when the United States was founded.

Today, 78% of the country's American Indians don't live in reservations (Wikipedia Contributors, 2019a). Currently, the states with the largest proportion of tribal people living are Alaska, New Mexico, Montana, and the Dakotas.

The rights and benefits that were stipulated in the treaties included a significant amount of tribal sovereignty or authority. This system is used throughout the tribal lands, and it works differently from the law of the U.S. states. American Indians aren't always allowed to vote in local, state, and federal elections, yet the law does provide protections in regard to the 14th Amendment. This means that the American Indian people are not taxed.

Most reservations are located West of the Mississippi River, where the Native population still stays and upholds their customs. Tribal Americans have become more aware of their values, customs, and culture and proudly uphold their culture. Tribes understand their roots and what beginnings they have come from.

Problems in the Reserves

In many reserves, there are serious issues such as unemployment, poverty, and addiction to alcohol and drugs. Another issue is the high level of American Indians with diabetes and heart disease. American tribal members are working with organizations that are trying to respect their traditions and incorporate Western medical benefits into their cultural practices.

Sometimes, however, when the government

tries to solve the issues, the opposite happens, and it worsens the situation rather than fixes it. The current five hundred and sixty-two tribes have the authority to establish their own governments, enforce laws (both civil and criminal), impose taxes, set membership standards, license, and control their own activities, zone their lands, and exclude people from their territories.

The very same restrictions that the U.S. government has enforced still apply to the tribal powers of self-governed land; for instance, neither governments nor tribes have the authority to wage war, engage in international relations, or create their own currency or money.

Yet, the U.S. continues to want to rule American tribal populations and treat them as though they were subject to U.S. law. Certain American Indian activists contend that the U.S. Federal Government must treat American tribal people as any other independent nation in order to really respect American Indian authority.

For instance, Native American advocates say it's disrespectful and humiliating for the U.S. to keep land 'in trust' and try to control it in any way - whether it be the Canadians, the U.S. Federal Government, or anyone who is a non-

American Indian body.

Yet, Americans respect independence and self-determination - as this emphasizes the importance of every person in determining their own identity and future with regard to their own decisions, effort, and skills.

Independence develops a person's capacity for self-reliance (depending on themselves) and self-sufficiency. This enables us as a whole to take the right actions in building happy lives for ourselves and our families.

Horse Riders Line-up at Little Bighorn

How Can We Support Native American Communities

The American Indians need help to improve their situation, and you can help them! Even if it's just to share in the awareness of their needs as the indigenous people of America. Encourage others around you to donate to the tribal communities.

Donate to the Communities

Several Indigenous organizations continue to seek increased acknowledgment of their identity and the right to speak for themselves in political debates. There are legal and cultural battles involved, but there are also resource battles taking place, and they need to be financed.

For example, the campaign to fund the Indigenous communities was pushed aside by Covid-19. Not only did the epidemic have extremely negative health effects on Indigenous populations, but it also caused the casino and tourism industries to collapse, which was an important source of tax money for many American Indians.

In saying all of this, we can donate funds to the American Indian communities. This will help them to pay for political issues that they need to resolve and for food shortages.

Buy and Support American Indian Work

As you know, the tribe's people are gifted in making pottery, weaving, and beading, and they also sell the produce that they farm. Why not buy what they sell, and tell everyone else to do the same?

Take Trips to Areas That Support the Tribes

Encourage your family and friends to go on outings and explore areas where the tribal people lived, hunted, gathered food, and worshiped. Entrance fees and funds, when going on these outings to the sacrificial tribal areas, often go towards the Hualapai communities, as this group is not funded by the government.

Organize Fundraisers

On 'Thanksgiving,' 'Indigenous People's Day,' or 'Heritage Month,' certain generous supporters donate the revenues from their businesses or organize NARF fundraising events. Ask your parents to speak to their company or workplace to support the American Tribal people in this way. You could also ask your school to help raise money through a raffle system. You might have another way of making people more aware, by posting something on Facebook.

Be a Diplomat

It's appreciated by millions when you represent NARF and spread the word about their battle for American tribal rights. You can share information at times about the ongoing efforts to end decades of discriminatory laws and, in this way, guarantee Native American rights.

The Native American Rights Fund's (NARF) mission is to hold governments accountable for their promises. The NARF uses litigation, legal advocacy, and expertise to defend Native American rights, resources, and the cultural way of life.

An elected board of directors oversees the nonprofit NARF, which consists of thirteen different tribes across the nation. These thirteen tribes have different levels of experience and knowledge of Native American issues. Five main areas below are seen as top priorities:

- Safeguard tribal natural resources and preserve tribal existence.
- Promote the rights of Native Americans.
- Holding the authorities liable for American tribes.
- Create American Indian law and inform the people about their issues and rights.

Since 1970, NARF has won hundreds of important lawsuits in key aspects, such as tribal independence, treaty rights, preservation of biodiversity, right to vote, and Indian education, thereby advancing and defending the Native American tribes' heritage.

While tribes use their sovereign right to manage their own affairs, their rights, resources, and ways of life are preserved and maintained; commitments that are made towards them are upheld, and they exercise their authority to handle their own affairs.

CONCLUSIONS

Most American Indians have lost their belief that the earth is sacred. Their entire culture and way of living have changed, causing physical, mental, and emotional issues within the tribes.

What do you do to protect the environment? Do you recycle or pick up paper and rubbish that's thrown around?

In the Tribal areas, ancestral voices are coming down the generations. They are saying, "Look after and handle the earth well, as you have not received the world from us; it's only on loan to you and those that follow in your footsteps."

How can we say that we love one another when we don't care for the land and everyone's future? We should also focus on the family as a whole and pull together in unity. The wisdom and traditions of a lost way of life need to be rediscovered and rekindled by parents of the next generation, who are discovering power in the old culture.

They understand that if they want to protect their children from the risks of despair, addiction, and suicide, they need to connect with the feelings and ways of the past. The children need to feel that same pride, honor, and goodwill–towards the earth and one another. Learning more about the past ways and beliefs will, in turn, ensure their success.

Do you, as a family, follow certain traditional concepts that are different from everyone else's in the U.S.?

There are ways to believe that you are a vital member of your tribe or community, and you have a purpose in this world. Healing comes from the ancient family ties that extended to every tribal member or otherwise. This is where your core strength will come from!

Having grandparents, uncles, nephews, cousins, or some mix of family members—all living together—raises a positive, strong generation with respect for everything and everyone around them is the way forward.

Don't you feel confident and relaxed when you have a lot of families around you? I believe you will think of yourself as part of a network of supportive people that extends beyond parents and siblings.

You will feel grounded and become one with the earth and nature again. This method has proved to be quite valuable for many American Indian children, especially those with parents that have adopted damaging habits such as addictions or any other bad behaviors.

There has, however, been improvement as more Americans are starting to reflect on the Native Americans' culture and the condition of the planet. Those that carry a Native American bloodline are realizing the importance of their heritage and moving back to their rich, full way of life. More of the tribes are learning to speak their original languages and are moving towards a positive lifestyle.

They are exercising and trying to eat correctly, as their ancestors did before them. Unfortunately, there are challenges or difficulties for some who live in reserve and have no way of transport to get to a fresh grocer. These tribal people have depended mostly on convenience stores, which has caused a lot of health problems, such as diabetes. Tribal groups have recently come together as they look for solutions to these health issues.

They have also come together in force against the Dakota Access Pipeline argument. The Oceti Sakowin tribe's people came in their thousands to rally in the town of Cannon Ball, which lies in a remote area of North Dakota. Together they stood against the installation of the pipeline because it was close to the river. The Standing Rock Sioux tribe worried about the river becoming polluted, and rightly so.

There are signs of hope as tribal people come together for the good of their continent. Lives all around the nation are changing for the better. A fresh wave of an uprising is beginning as the reclaiming of past ways and ideas is being accepted and sprung to life. Tribal people are asking, what would my ancestors do?

Tales, as well as stories of myths, are being picked up and shared. The telling of memorable tales is at the heart of this new surge of leadership, optimism, or positiveness, and healing is taking hold.

Why tell stories? Because sharing the struggles and victories or triumphs of Native people might be that strong force that generations need to receive, healing can start, and personal growth and unity can begin in a big way.

There is still so much that needs to be done; finances and fundraising are needed to fuel the process. So, tribes in the twenty-first century can keep fighting wars against people who are trying to destroy the land and their heritage. You can start by becoming a diplomat and exchange stories and hopes for the future through modern technology.

It's vital that a complete rediscovery occurs so that the ancient oral traditions are upheld. The true spirit of the indigenous tribal people can rise within this generation to remove any barriers, so problems can be resolved. This will allow a future to be grafted from past successes.

The American Indians believe that they should be strong enough to stand alone and be themselves enough to stand apart. Yet, they should also be wise enough to stand together when the time comes (White, 2022).

Everyone is invited to connect in the process of listening, understanding, and reflecting on these ancient pasts. To see how the indigenous people lived, we can consider the state of our lives and the journey of others by working together to save this beautiful planet.

If you loved learning or rediscovering, and you found this book interesting, drop me a message. I am interested in your views.

REFERENCES

Acemoglu, D., Johnson, S., & Robinson, J. A. (2001). The colonial origins of comparative development: An empirical investigation. American Economic Review, 91(5), 1369–1401.

Biskinik Newspaper, S. (2022). By kendra germany-wall. In Biskinik Newspaper. https://www.choctawnation.com/wp-content/uploads/2022/05/apr2022-biskinik.pdf

C & D Gifts Native American Art, S. (2022, April 15). What Native American tribes made pottery? C & D Gifts Native American Art. https://canddgiftsnm.com/blogs/news/what-Native-american-tribes-made-pottery

CA State Parks. (n.d.). American Indian basketry. CA State Parks. https://www.parks.ca.gov/?page_id=24166#:~:text=Baskets%20were%20used%20for%20utilitarian

Chahira, K. (2008, December 1). Ancient skeletal evidence: Topics by science.gov. Science. https://www.science.gov/topicpages/a/ancient+skeletal+evidence

Claydon, J. (n.d.). Origin & history. World Lacrosse. https://worldlacrosse.sport/about/origin-history/#:~:text=Lacrosse%20was%20started%20by%20the

Crow Canyon. (2023, March 28). Navajo indians today | peoples of mesa verde. Crow Canyon. https://www.crowcanyon.org/educationproducts/peoples_mesa_verde/today_navajo.asp#:~:text=Today%3A%20Mid%2D1900s%20to%20the%20Present&text=(See%20enlarged%20photograph.)

Cyca, M. (2022, October 4). 9 facts about Native American tribes. History. https://www.history.com/news/Native-american-tribes-facts

Drexler, K. (2019, January 22). Research guides: Indian

removal act: Primary documents in american history: Introduction. Guides Local Government. https://guides.loc.gov/indian-removal-act

National Parks Traveler. (n.d.). Did the first europeans to see the grand canyon leave this mysterious inscription? National Parks Traveler. Retrieved April 10, 2023, from https://www.nationalparkstraveler.org/2010/11/did-first-europeans-see-grand-canyon-leave-mysterious-inscription7243

Encyclopædia Britannica. (2019). Igloo | dwelling. In Encyclopædia Britannica. https://www.britannica.com/technology/igloo

Filice, M. (2018, July 19). Country food inuit food in canada | the canadian encyclopedia. Www.thecanadianencyclopedia.ca. https://www.thecanadianencyclopedia.ca/en/article/country-food-inuit-food-in-canada#:~:text=The%20Inuit%20harvest%2C%20trap%2C%20hunt

Germany, W. K. (2022). In Biskinik Newspaper. https://www.choctawnation.com/wp-content/uploads/2022/05/apr2022-biskinik.pdf

Grimm, D. (2018, July 5). America's first dogs lived with people for thousands of years. Then they vanished. Science. https://www.science.org/content/article/america-s-first-dogs-lived-people-thousands-years-then-they-vanished#:~:text=Then%20they%20vanished-

History. (2023, March 12). Young Cynthia Anne Parker kidnapped during Native American raid. History. https://www.history.com/this-day-in-history/cynthia-ann-parker-is-kidnapped#:~:text=In%20the%20chaos%2C%20the%20Native,for%20the%20next%2025%20years.

Medlineplus. (n.d.). Livedo reticularis: MedlinePlus medical encyclopedia. Medlineplus. https://medlineplus.gov/ency/article/001478.htm

National Clothing, S. (2018, March 15). Traditional

braiding of Native american indians. how to weave without a loom - nationalclothing.org. National Clothing. https://nationalclothing.org/america/81-Native-american-indians/242-traditional-braiding-of-Native-american-indians-how-to-weave-without-a-loom.html

National Parks Traveler. (n.d.). Did the first europeans to see the grand canyon leave this mysterious inscription? National Parks Traveler. Retrieved April 10, 2023, from https://www.nationalparkstraveler.org/2010/11/did-first-europeans-see-grand-canyon-leave-mysterious-inscription7243

NDLA, S. (2019, January 31). Native americans today. NDLA. https://ndla.no/en/subject:1:4ad7fe49-b14a-4caf-8e19-ad402d1e2ce6/topic:1:b9b98bf8-787d-4d25-a0c6-37c725050502/topic:1:e3bbd497-8bb6-4654-a970-9106cd69e178/resource:1:6203

Orlega, N. (2020, November 5). Native american: Shinny to hockey – mass appeal. Mass Appeal. https://massappealmagazine.com/Native-american-shinny-to-hockey/

Science Daily, S. (2015, September 17). Adaptation to high-fat diet, cold had profound effect on inuit, including shorter height: Greenlanders developed unique mutations to deal with diet high in omega-3 fatty acids. Science Daily. https://www.sciencedaily.com/releases/2015/09/150917160034.htm

Smithers, G. D. (2015, October 1). Why do so many americans think they have cherokee blood? Slate Magazine. https://slate.com/news-and-politics/2015/10/cherokee-blood-why-do-so-many-americans-believe-they-have-cherokee-ancestry.html

Snow, D. (2008, March 28). The first americans and the differentiation of hunter-gatherer cultures (B. G. Trigger & W. E. Washburn, Eds.). Cambridge

State Museum Arizona. (n.d.). Hot chocolate cylinder jar

| arizona state museum. State Museum Arizona. Retrieved April 10, 2023, from https://statemuseum.arizona.edu/online-exhibit/curators-choice/hot-chocolate-cylinder-jar

University Press. https://www.cambridge.org/core/books/abs/cambridge-history-of-the-Native-peoples-of-the-americas/first-americans-and-the-differentiation-of-huntergatherer-cultures/4AEC5568ED152664E618486ECB22AAFE

Stebbins, S. (2017). Pocahontas: Her life and legend - historic jamestowne part of colonial national historical park (U.S. national park service). NPS GOV. https://www.nps.gov/jame/learn/historyculture/pocahontas-her-life-and-legend.htm

The Canadian Encyclopedia, S. (n.d.). Country food inuit food in canada | the canadian encyclopedia. The Canadian Encyclopedia. https://www.thecanadianencyclopedia.ca/en/article/country-food-inuit-food-in-canada#:~:text=The%20Inuit%20harvest%2C%20trap%2C%20hunt

UNC Greensboro. (n.d.). Inuit of utkuhikhalik and qipisa communities | peaceful societies. UNC Greensboro. Retrieved March 25, 2023, https://peacefulsocieties.uncg.edu/societies/inuit/#:~:text=They%20exhibit%20very%20little%20tension

USA Government, S. (n.d.). Indian tribes and resources for Native americans | usagov. USA Government. https://www.usa.gov/tribes#:~:text=for%20Native%20Americans-

White, S. (2022, January 25). Pin on quotes. Pinterest. https://za.pinterest.com/pin/1055599890644081/

Wikipedia. (2020, May 26). Montreal lacrosse club. Wikipedia. https://en.wikipedia.org/wiki/Montreal_Lacrosse_Club

Wikipedia. (2022, October 16). Native american religions.

Wikipedia. https://en.wikipedia.org/wiki/Native_American_religions#:~:text=Early%20European%20explorers%20describe%20individual

Wikipedia Contributors. (2018, November 19). Pocahontas. Wikipedia. https://en.wikipedia.org/wiki/Pocahontas

Wikipedia Contributors. (2019a, April 4). Eskimo. Wikipedia. https://en.wikipedia.org/wiki/Eskimo

Wikipedia Contributors. (2019c, March 4). Sacagawea. Wikipedia. https://en.wikipedia.org/wiki/Sacagawea

Wikipedia Contributors. (2019b, June 10). Shinny. Wikipedia. https://en.wikipedia.org/wiki/Shinnyhttps://en.wikipedia.org/wiki/Sitting_Bull

Wikipedia Contributors. (2019f, August 4). Sitting bull. Wikipedia. https://en.wikipedia.org/wiki/Sitting_Bull

Wikipedia Contributors. (2019g, December 17). Colorado river. Wikipedia. https://en.wikipedia.org/wiki/Colorado_River

Wikipedia, S. (2023, January 5). Bernardo de miera y pacheco. Wikipedia. https://en.wikipedia.org/wiki/Bernardo_de_Miera_y_Pacheco

Image References

Rivat, A. (2017, August 1). Grand canyon. Unsplash. https://unsplash.com/photos/zGnXou4siEI

Alexander, R. (2022, July 26). American bison. Pixabay. https://pixabay.com/photos/bison-american-bison-buffalo-wild-7342765/

Ann, T. (n.d.). Inuit craft. Pixabay. https://pixabay.com/photos/figurine-native-eskimo-sculpture-7515317/

James, A. (2018, June 29). Lakota native american man at pow wow. Unsplash. https://unsplash.com/photos/ehdsg7SHm6A

Bertrand. (2018, February 1). Photo by bertrand borie on

unsplash. Unsplash. https://unsplash.com/photos/CqyXj895IUg

Brown, R. (n.d.). Native-american-pottery-clay-jugs. Pixabay. https://pixabay.com/photos/native-american-pottery-clay-jugs-952392/

Blunk-Fernández, D. (2021, May 4). Native american horse riders line up at little big horn. Unsplash. https://unsplash.com/photos/Oa2qHtJdoCI

De Bruin, E. (n.d.). Rust color statue. Pixabay. https://pixabay.com/photos/image-rust-rust-color-1574835/

Diapicard. (n.d.). Igloo snow house. Pixabay. https://pixabay.com/photos/igloo-snow-house-landscape-ice-1114042/

Dowd, D. (2020, March 12). Indigenious american. Pixabay. https://pixabay.com/images/search/indigenious%20american%20headpieces/?manual_search=1

Ince, C. (2020, January 10). Native beaded-moccasins. Pixabay. https://pixabay.com/photos/beaded-moccasins-regalia-native-1787140/

Demeester, I. (2021, February 13). Inuit sled dogs near kimmirut, nunavut. Unsplash. https://unsplash.com/photos/r2D9KtPg7_o

Johnson, G. (2022, February 27). Thanksgiving-feast-painting. Pixabay. https://pixabay.com/vectors/thanksgiving-feast-painting-5616807/

Linder, R. (2022, September 25). Basket weave. Unsplash. https://unsplash.com/photos/kiOntIZ_rMQ

Elmoutassir, T. (2022, July 16). ptarmigans bird. Unsplash. https://unsplash.com/photos/7vL48HdzXmU

Grote, T. (2017, October 17). Sioux man in the city. Unsplash. https://unsplash.com/photos/rnH5ITofDAM

Tom, H. (2020a, March 16). Chiricahua apache, 1898. Unsplash. https://unsplash.com/photos/rGMJSvfmAU

Unsplash. (2020b, March 16). Turning eagle sioux 1898. Unsplash. https://unsplash.com/photos/KR1vgTni7W4

Unsplash. (2020c, March 16). Two little crows 1898. Unsplash. https://unsplash.com/photos/b11E0M88T3U

Bentt, W (2021, June 8). Fabulous cliff dwellings at mesa verde. Unsplash. https://unsplash.com/photos/zztLOhvnHNk

FREE BONUS FROM HBA: EBOOK BUNDLE

Greetings!

First of all, thank you for reading our books. As fellow passionate readers of History and Mythology, we aim to create the very best books for our readers.

Now, we invite you to join our VIP list. As a welcome gift, we offer the History & Mythology Ebook Bundle below for free. Plus you can be the first to receive new books and exclusives! <u>Remember it's 100% free to join.</u>

Simply scan the QR code to join.

OTHER BOOKS BY HISTORY BROUGHT ALIVE

Available now in Ebook, Paperback, Hardcover, and Audiobook in all regions.

For Kids:

NATIVE AMERICAN HISTORY FOR KIDS

We sincerely hope you enjoyed our new book ***"Native American for Kids"***. We would greatly appreciate your feedback with an honest review at the place of purchase.

First and foremost, we are always looking to grow and improve as a team. It is reassuring to hear what works, as well as receive constructive feedback on what should improve. Second, starting out as an unknown author is exceedingly difficult, and Amazon reviews go a long way toward making the journey out of anonymity possible. Please take a few minutes to write an honest review.

Best regards,
History Brought Alive
http://historybroughtalive.com/

www.ingramcontent.com/pod-product-compliance
Lightning Source LLC
Chambersburg PA
CBHW070553010526
44118CB00012B/1309